THE LORD'S SUPPER
IN THE NEW TESTAMENT

Society of Biblical Literature

History of Biblical Studies

L. L. Welborn
New Testament Editor

Number 1

The Lord's Supper in the New Testament
by Albert Eichhorn

THE LORD'S SUPPER
IN THE NEW TESTAMENT

by Albert Eichhorn

With an introductory essay by Hugo Gressmann,
"Albert Eichhorn and the History of Religion School"

Translated by Jeffrey F. Cayzer

Society of Biblical Literature
Atlanta

THE LORD'S SUPPER IN THE NEW TESTAMENT

Library of Congress Cataloging-in-Publication Data

Eichhorn, Albert, 1856–1926.
    [Abendmahl im Neuen Testament. English]
    The Lord's Supper in the New Testament / by Albert Eichhorn ; with an introductory essay by Hugo Gressmann, "Albert Eichhorn and the history of religion school" ; translated by Jeffrey F. Cayzer.
        p. cm. — (Society of Biblical Literature history of biblical studies ; no. 1)
    Includes bibliographical references and indexes.
    ISBN: 978-1-58983-274-9 (pbk. : alk. paper)
    1. Lord's Supper—Biblical teaching. 2. Bible. N.T.—Criticism, interpretation, etc. 3. Eichhorn, Albert, 1856–1926. 4. Religionsgeschichtliche Schule. I. Gressmann, Hugo, 1877–1927. Albert Eichhorn und die Religionsgeschichtliche Schule. English. II. Title.
    BS2545.L58E33 2007b
    234'.16309015—dc22   2007035584

15 14 13 12 11 10 09 08 07   5 4 3 2 1
Printed in the United States of America on acid-free, recycled paper conforming to ANSI/NISO Z39.48-1992 (R1997) and ISO 9706:1994 standards for paper permanence.

Contents

Editor's Foreword

It is fitting that the new SBLHBS series should be inaugurated by the publication of Albert Eichhorn's *The Lord's Supper in the New Testament*, together with an introductory essay by Hugo Gressmann on "Albert Eichhorn and the History of Religion School." Albert Eichhorn was acknowledged as the "first among equals" by a group of scholars assembled at Göttingen in the 1880s committed to a new method in the investigation of Christianity as a religion among other religions, as a means of liberation from dogma and canon. Among the members of this group (which included Hermann Gunkel, William Wrede, and Wilhelm Bousset), Eichhorn played the role of the Socratic midwife, posing fundamental questions about the origins of Christian theology and nurturing discoveries by his younger colleagues through sustained, critical dialogue. Eichhorn's penetrating analysis of the Lord's Supper traditions in the New Testament, one of the few works he published before the onset of illness, exemplifies the qualities for which he was so highly prized by his colleagues and students: the sure ability to distinguish layers of tradition within the text, the full appreciation of the role of early Christian worship in shaping the reports about Jesus' life, the forthright acknowledgement of the difficulty of ascertaining the original historical events, the unflinching recognition of the influence of Near Eastern and Hellenistic religions upon Christian tradition, even in its earliest stages.

Thus Eichhorn is the ideal mentor for the audience for whom this new series is intended: a rising generation of scholars and graduate students from diverse cultural contexts who are entering into the global discourse about the future of biblical studies at a time when English is rapidly replacing German as the international language of scholarship. It is hoped that Eichhorn's passionate commitment to the investigation of early Christianity in its ancient cultural and religious contexts will inspire a new generation of scholars who are attempting, now increasingly from a postcolonial perspective, to draw substantive comparisons between the faith and worship of the early Christians and the religion and cultus of the Roman Empire.

As the New Testament editor of SBLHBS, I wish to thank my colleague, Leo Perdue, for inviting me to join him in this enterprise, my friend Jeffrey Cayzer for his elegant and richly annotated translation, and my teacher Gerd Lüdemann for modeling the dedication to historical research that characterized the history of religion school and for suggesting that Eichhorn's monograph should be the first publication in the series.

L. L. Welborn
Professor of New Testament and Early Christianity
Fordham University

TRANSLATOR'S PREFACE

In preparing the translation of these two works, I have been aware of the changes in German and in English style that have taken place in the last century since these booklets were written. I have tried to capture something of the formality of the period without sacrificing the main aim, which is to produce English that reads like English (not a translation from German) and is acceptable to a modern reader.

In accordance with this broad aim, which is my usual one in translating German theological works, some terms are translated in quite different ways, according to the context. An example of this is *Spekulationen*, for which the renderings vary as widely as "the possibilities of interpretation" and "mere conjecture."

The German term *das Abendmahl*, preferred by both Gressmann and Eichhorn, has almost invariably been translated as the Lord's Supper, but at times I have used Communion for variety where it seemed not to risk confusion. The standard translation of Luther's *Works* uses both terms, as well as Mass and Christ's Supper, but Lord's Supper is the most common overall. This term is also used in common English translations of 1 Cor 11 and is in frequent use in a range of Protestant churches.

Explanatory notes have been added to both texts and are enclosed in square brackets [ ]. In the case of Gressmann's work, these are numerous, principally to provide brief information about almost all of the personalities of the era he mentions. My sources for these notes have chiefly been online: the *Biographisches-Bibliographisches Kirchenlexikon* (http://www.bautz.de/bbkl/), *Grimms Wörterbuch* (http://germazope.uni-trier.de/Projects/WBB/woerterbuecher/dwb/wbgui?lemid+GA00001), and at times the various encyclopedias. I mention these sources in gratitude to all those who have put so much effort into making them readily available and to remind those who read this translation where they will most quickly find additional information.

In addition, some material from the body of Gressmann's work is occasionally transferred to footnotes. This is usually when a quote or a digression would interrupt the flow of meaning. As an aid for the reader who may like to compare, the page numbers from the original German documents are supplied in the body of the text, enclosed within square brackets.

Jeffrey F. Cayzer
Sydney, October 2006

ALBERT EICHHORN AND THE HISTORY OF RELIGION SCHOOL

by Hugo Gressmann

Originally published as *Albert Eichhorn und Die Religions-geschichtliche Schule.* Göttingen: Vandenhoeck & Ruprecht, 1914.

[iii] PREFACE

Who is Albert Eichhorn? How many people have heard his name, but how few know anything about him! He has never written any books, yet he will be remembered not only by the innumerable friends who will be eternally grateful to him, but he will also go down in the history of theological scholarship, which has entered him in the Book of Life along with the history of religion school.

It is precisely because he cannot receive sufficient recognition from the brief essays he has published that I have considered it my duty to describe what he is like for those who have no knowledge of him, so that they may have a clear picture and gain an accurate impression.

Now, the external events that impinge upon our lives are normally just a shell that covers the person on the inside, but when they are what fundamentally determines who someone is, they are always essential for gaining an understanding. And when the paths of well-known people cross, biography arouses the interest of a broader circle.

So, while following the main dates in chronological order, I have been careful to interweave fate and character, together with the threads that connect Eichhorn to his contemporaries. However, it was also my wish to do complete justice to the life of this one man and to this period of history. Therefore it seemed essential to fit this particular segment into the latest movement in scholarly theology and to place the personal element into the larger historical context of scholarship. Anyone wanting to measure Eichhorn's importance must also be clear about what goes to make up the history of religion school. I was not concerned to provide an exhaustive treatment of the work of this school and an objective judgment of its achievements—the time is not yet ripe for that. Rather, I wished to depict plainly its general method and the main outline of its development.

A great number of scholars have flocked to my assistance in this project, and I have been grateful to make use of the information and encouragement they have provided both orally and in writing. I should mention in particular Professors Gunkel and Baumgarten, to whose names must be added those of Professors Bremer, Geffcken, Mulert, Troeltsch, Wobbermin, and Zimmern, as well as Mrs. Wrede.

Hugo Gressmann

[1] I said, "I will water my garden
and drench my flowerbeds,"
And lo, my canal became a river
and my river a sea.
Observe that I have not labored for myself alone,
but for all who seek wisdom.

Sirach 24:31, 34

1. Albert Eichhorn

Karl Albert August Ludwig Eichhorn was born on the first of October 1856 as the son of a pastor in Garlsdorf near Lüneburg. Until he was fifteen he was taught by his father. From Michaelmas term 1871 until Easter 1875 he went to school at the Andreanum Gymnasium in Hildesheim, after which he devoted himself to the study of theology at Leipzig to Easter 1876, in Erlangen to Easter 1877, and in Göttingen until Michaelmas 1878, when he passed his first examination. After that he spent a year in Riede helping his ailing father, who had been posted there in 1870. In Michaelmas term 1879 he was accepted at the college in Loccum, where he spent a year and a half receiving a superb academic and practical education. At Easter 1881 he passed the second theology examination and was appointed as a curate by the *Landeskonsistorium*, the church board of that state. His first posting after ordination was to act as temporary second minister in Bergen near Celle, but after only three months he was without further ado entrusted with the full office of pastor in Riede, alongside his father. He remained there until his father's retirement in 1884 (the latter died only ten months later), when he received permission to leave pastoral ministry and prepare himself for an academic calling.

[2] Eichhorn was a product of and maintained a certain affection for the Hanoverian Lutheran orthodoxy, despite the fact that they wanted nothing to do with him. This is where he also gained his understanding and deep familiarity with living religion, which meant more to him than

just an interesting research topic. Being himself of a profound and gentle religious nature, he could never attack a different religious position and was not dissuaded by dogmatic controversy from profiting from those who held other opinions than his own. Later he frequented the church of the venerable orthodox pastor H. Hoffmann, a man who lived by and lived out traditional church beliefs, a unique character who felt free to use humor in the pulpit; educated men and women flocked to the warm welcome of his church in Neumarkt.

Eichhorn was just as regular in attending worship at the church of his friend Baumgarten[1] in Kiel. Having left pastoral ministry principally to preserve his public and private independence, he also continued to maintain his distance from church politics, considering that his circle of friends was simply *Die Christliche Welt*[2] and, at least in his earlier years, frequenting their gatherings. Likewise, he found all political parties repugnant, despite happily engaging with politics and political issues. Even when abroad, he never denied his love for his homeland and often stressed the advantages of Hanover over Prussia, albeit with a humor tinged with irony. He was particularly proud of Hanover's lawyers and administrators, yet he was no Guelph[3] in the political sense. He placed the highest value on the National Liberals, or at least on some of the far-sighted individuals in the party, without being blind to the weaknesses of the party as a whole. His feeling for justice showed in his constant support for whichever party was not in power. His need for objectivity is seen in his subscribing simultaneously to the extremist publications *Kreuzzeitung* and *Vorwärts*.[4] When the postmaster read the subscription note he hurried off to see Eichhorn in person in order to apologize for this "error" of his subordinate. Eichhorn

---

1. [Otto Baumgarten (1858–1934) was a theologian, Professor of Practical Theology in Kiel, and leader of the theological "left" who struggled for various reforms in the Protestant church.]

2. [See note 55 below.]

3. [The house of Guelph (*die Welfen; das Welfenhaus*) was the ancient ruling family in Hanover (and the royal family in Britain from 1714 to 1837) until deposed by the Prussians in 1866. To call someone a Guelph was to imply that the person was a lover of all things to do with Hanover's traditions.]

4. [The *Kreuzzeitung* (*Neue Preussische Zeitung*) was established in Prussia in 1848 as a voice for ultra-conservative opinion. *Vorwärts* was the name of more than one radical publication of the left; the reference here is most likely to the main publication of the Social Democratic Party of Germany in the 1890s.]

took great delight in recounting how hard it had been to convince the gentleman that there was no error.

He generally considered liberalism in church and politics to be somewhat unproductive, but since he was a merciless critic of all prejudice, even on the conservative and orthodox side, he also remained an outsider in politics and in the church and felt very comfortable in that role.

[3] We may see, typically, how hard he was on himself and how modest he was about his abilities in the fact that he still preached on occasion in Halle, but only in the early services that few pastors were in the habit of attending. We may consider as a fruit of his practical endeavors a talk[5] that caused quite a fuss: "Some Thoughts on Preaching." Here he describes, not without a certain humor, the various kinds of preachers he has met in his regular visits to churches. He begins with the orthodox Lutheran type—familiar to him—who stresses the authority of the Bible and justification by faith without works and who at the same time rails against the unbelief of the Protestant Union. These were highly principled, mass-produced items with no independent ideas.

Then he adds the arrogant liberal superintendent who touches on the text in the broadest and most superficial way and whose "liberal thoughts do no real harm, since he has no thought at all." A third type of preacher is the well-trained technician who follows the dictates of conventional homiletics and devotes seven minutes to the "noble" content, seven minutes to the application for us. Just the theme of the mother at the bedside of her sick child takes up two minutes. The advantage of such a sermon is that it can be produced at any time on demand without any preparation.

The fourth kind is the golden-tongued preacher who loves to expatiate fervently and imbue every sentence with profound feeling, convinced that he is speaking directly to the heart, "and the congregation thinks so too." What this orator lacks in ideas he makes up for in clichés.

The fifth kind of preacher stands in contrast: the dogmatician who has ideas in abundance and dresses them up not one whit. However, he fails to involve the congregation because he delivers theological lectures, justifying his theological position to an audience of theologians and because his attacks on orthodoxy never reach any further than that same target.

---

5. Later published as "Etwas vom Predigen" in *Die Christliche Welt* (1895), cols. 273–76, 308–10.

"He misses the point that you only have doubts about the teachings of the church if you are still inwardly bound by them."

The sixth kind is the worst. He has set his heart on the things of the old church tradition and on whatever is unsettling to people of today. [4] "It is a naïve idea worthy of scorn to think that something extinct and incomprehensible could be made lively and intelligible to us by proving that hundreds of years ago it was alive and reasonable."

Not content with outlining the main kinds of preacher, Eichhorn shows us in each case where the error lies and in so doing adds a positive element to the negative. So he gives the example of what a preacher should be like, choosing as an example the sermon of an unnamed friend. It is not hard to guess who is being referred to here.

First, Eichhorn tells us to avoid all clichés (and here he agrees with Wrede): "Blessed are those who utter no clichés, for they shall be understood." It is not only the gushings and well-meaning contortions of the orator he is against, as, carried away by his enthusiasm, he wrongly attributes false motives to others. Eichhorn is also attacking the conventional nuggets of wisdom inherited from the preacher's forebears and worn down into trite worthlessness by repeated use.

For Eichhorn the highest virtue is truth, not the truth of centuries gone by, but the truth of people of today. Once we knew only of the simplistic contrasts between good and evil, pious and godless; now we are aware of shades of meaning and demand relative standards. "If the preacher has no awareness, then the best and most profound things come out as mere clichés." His inherent faithfulness to the truth is seen in his taking the time to reflect on the problems himself, in the fact that it is his own ideas that provide the impulse, and in his not simply reproducing the set stock of commentaries and sermon collections.

It is not possible to hold the attention of people of today if you take well-worn paths in your preaching and even your liturgy, if you run on the tracks of tradition with none of your own freedom to range more widely, or if you insist on waging useless wars against defeated theological positions. If churches are not to keep on emptying, then sermons must hold people's attention. So the general rule is not to remain stuck in the mud, preaching the same old three-point sermons Sunday after Sunday to assembled Christendom. Nor should you proffer opinions that no one shares or, conversely, ignore views held by everyone today. If you lose touch with the present, then the sermon has lost its effect by the end of the service. [5] If only great numbers of pastors and above all those studying to be preachers thought through and took to heart Eichhorn's arguments, which are still valid today.

At Easter 1884, Eichhorn returned to Göttingen, where he spent a year and a half preparing his master's thesis. There he fell in with a group of younger theologians; he had a lively interchange with them and even then, without intending to, held them enthralled with his abundance of ideas. Members of this group included Wrede, Gunkel, Mirbt, Bornemann, the philologist Geffcken, and the philosopher Külpe; some of these took an active interest in his ideas.[6] Even the younger students testified to a lasting impression of how original he was as a human being as well as a scholar. They spoke of his clear and keen sense of history, even if they did not always understand what he was saying. The impulsive ones no doubt took offense at him; they were uneasy and even put out when he asked them whether Jesus had really been raised from the dead—a question that tallied so poorly with Ritschl's theology—and then expected a clear answer! It was not only Gunkel and others he helped to free themselves from Ritschl; even Troeltsch confessed: "It seemed to me that Ritschl's combining of ideas about religion that are valid and suitable for today was done without sufficient regard to the hard-won results of historical research that stood as fundamentally complete, even considering the questions that still remain open. The latter impression was strengthened by the influence that such outstanding philologists and historians as Lagarde, Wellhausen, Duhm, Smend, Jülicher, and Eichhorn had on us."[7]

---

6. [Hermann Gunkel (1862–1932), Professor of Old Testament in Berlin, Giessen, and Halle, was one of the main representatives of the history of religion school and pioneered form and genre research in the Old Testament. From the beginning, he was a major collaborator and advisor to the first edition and became co-editor of the second edition of *RGG*. Carl Mirbt (1860–1929) was a church historian and missiologist. Wilhelm Bornemann (1858–1946) was a theologian and translator of Augustine's *Confessions*. Johannes Geffcken (1861–1935) was author of such works as *Griechische Literaturgeschichte*, *Der Ausgang des griechisch-römischen Heidentums* (*The Last Days of Greco-Roman Paganism*), and *Aus der Werdezeit des Christentums* and of many studies on early Christian literature. Oswald Külpe (1862–1915), philosopher and structural psychologist, was a professor at Würzburg.]

7. Ernst Troeltsch, *Das Historische in Kants Religionsphilosophie* (Berlin: Reuter & Reichard, 1904), vii.

Eichhorn's position on Ritschl at that time can be clearly seen in the three dogmatic theses that he defended for his doctorate in Halle.[8] No doubt all good Ritschlians shook their heads in disbelief at such statements as these:

Number 7: "The concepts of church and tradition are interchangeable."

Number 8: "The local congregation has no religious significance for the individual."

Number 8: "Dogmatics is not independent of either metaphysics or history."

In Göttingen, Eichhorn formed a lifelong friendship with the admirable and charming William Wrede, three years his junior. Wrede, at that time superintendent of the theological college, was a thoroughly genuine person, a born intellectual. It is true that they were later separated and did not see each other again for any length of time—[6] Eichhorn went to Halle, then Kiel; Wrede was called to Breslau, where he stayed until his death in 1906—but both men, with the similarity in their points of view and the way they developed, maintained a regular connection through

---

[Julius Wellhausen (1844–1918), orientalist, exegete, and historian, was one of the foremost scholars in Germany in the nineteenth century. His name is perhaps best known today for the Graf-Wellhausen hypothesis of the textual origins of the Hebrew Bible. Bernhard Duhm (1847–1928) was principally interested in the poetic and prophetic books of the Old Testament; his main achievement was tracing the development of prophecy in Israel. Rudolf Smend (1851–1913) was an Old Testament theologian. Adolf Jülicher (1857–1938), New Testament and church history specialist and professor in Marburg, was best known for his *Introduction to the New Testament* and most particularly for his massive two-volume study of the parables, *Die Gleichnisreden Jesu*, which spans almost 1,000 pages. Although all serious works on the parables since its publication in 1886 and 1899 have had to interact with its central thesis, it has never been translated into English.]

8. [Albrecht Ritschl (1822–1889), was one of the most influential Protestant systematic theologians of the nineteenth century. He developed his own theological system in his three-volume work *Die christliche Lehre von der Rechtfertigung und Versöhnung* (1870–1874), one volume of which was published as *The Christian Doctrine of Justification and Reconciliation: The Positive Development of the Doctrine* (ed. H. R. Mackintosh and A. B. Macaulay; New York: Scribner's, 1900). Influenced by Kant and Schleiermacher, his own pupils in turn included Harnack. His ideas on such topics as ethics and the kingdom of God, together with his refusal to place any value on eschatology, have tended to polarize other scholars, both during his lifetime and since.]

frequent brief reunions in Halle, Breslau, and elsewhere and through a lively correspondence.

They were both unashamedly Hanoverians, with an exceptional sense of their history, but they were also, as Jülicher correctly stresses, with all their differences, "kindred spirits" in their unflinching love of truth and the inexorable critique they brought to bear on all authorities, not least on themselves, because of their need for real clarity and because they were frankly modest about what it is possible to know for certain. This was the particular feature of the pamphlet that appeared anonymously in 1888 under the title *Im Kampf um die Weltanschauung* [*The Struggle for a Worldview*] that made him send it to all his friends, even Lagarde.

Neither Eichhorn nor Wrede was afraid of someone who knew nothing; on the contrary, in such an admission of ignorance they both recognized knowledge of the highest order. Eichhorn had a practiced eye for the various layers that overlie each other in the New Testament tradition and no doubt required even then that every scholar also have a sharp eye for spotting the period when every literary work was produced. Geffcken tells me that such an emphasis became particularly important for the work of Wrede, who made no secret of the fact that Eichhorn had had a decisive influence on the manner and direction of his thinking. Any attempt at demonstrating this influence is bound to fail, because Wrede's writings are completely independent of Eichhorn. Even his book *The Messianic Secret*,[9] which he dedicated to his "friend and teacher," was discussed by the two men only after its publication. Only in one place does Wrede specifically call attention to his dependence on Eichhorn, and even here he does not quote him directly.[10]

Conversely, if Wrede did admit he had been Eichhorn's pupil, it is only fair that we also describe him as Eichhorn's teacher, since the latter gained enormously from the penetrating and forceful way that Wrede expressed [7] problems and points of view. The finest thing about the lively exchange of ideas between the two men was the fact that neither kept accounts of what he had given and what he had received.

---

9. William Wrede, *Das Messiasgeheimnis in den Evangelien* (Göttingen: Vandenhoeck & Ruprecht, 1901), translated by J. C. Greig as *The Messianic Secret* (Greenwood, S.C.: Attic, 1971).

10. "Here I can in substance only repeat what Eichhorn has done in *Das Abendmahl im Neuen Testament* (1898). But my remarks have a somewhat different point" (Wrede, *Messianic Secret*, 88; cf. 272).

In the autumn of 1885 Eichhorn went to Halle with the intention of studying for the *Habilitation*[11] in church history. The chief aim of his thesis, written in Latin,[12] was to demonstrate the authenticity of the document *The Life of St. Anthony*, which gives important information on the origin of monasticism. Weingarten had denied that the document was written by Athanasius: "As clearly as the external witnesses appear to speak for the authorship of Athanasius, the internal testimony against that authorship is just as clear; it is the genuine writings of Athanasius that provide this contrary evidence."[13] Eichhorn took the contrary position, carefully examining the tradition and showing that Weingarten had overlooked many of the comments made by Athanasius and had misunderstood others. Eichhorn's convincing refutation today enjoys almost universal approval, and even his dating of the *Vita* to around 357 is accepted by most scholars. In an appendix he defended the authenticity of the *Historia Arianorum ad monachos* and demonstrated that it must have been written by Athanasius about 358—another accurate claim.

Although the quality of Eichhorn's scholarship and keen intellect were evident in this display of erudition, as to the extent of his grasp of the basic issues there was still some doubt, at least among those who knew little of the man. However, all reservations that might have been held in this regard were dispelled when on the sixth of July 1886 he defended his twenty-four theses in public disputation. Among them there are some that depart from the normal plan of things and are typical, not only of Eichhorn's bold manner, a manner that invited challenge, but also of the breadth of his vision and maturity of his judgment. So, for example, number 5 runs: "The task of a lecture on exegesis is not to exegete but to show how exegesis is to be done."

Two years later, on 3 November 1888, in the same place Baumgarten made an audacious statement, one that it is particularly interesting to compare with Eichhorn's: [8] "The reading of commentaries has the effect of spoiling a real, living and sensitive study of the Scriptures." Among Eichhorn's further theses we may mention:

---

11. [The *Habilitation* is the second doctoral thesis produced by candidates for university posts in Germany.]

12. *Athanasii de vita ascetica testimonia collecta* (Halle, 1886).

13. Hermann Weingarten, *Zeitschrift für Kirchengeschichte* 1 (1876): 10ff. [Weingarten (1834–92) was Professor of Church History at Marburg, then Breslau.]

Number 11: "Any interpretation of a myth that does not give due weight to its origin and development is a false one."

Number 12: "The writing of history is an art."

Number 14: "The basic rule for all historical research of individual items is never to approach by posing individual questions but always to start with the whole sphere to which the individual question belongs. Since the larger tasks can only be carried out by cooperative endeavor, what is needed is an organization of all scholarly efforts combined. Learned journals cannot replace such an organization."

Number 18: "Any consideration of church history from a religious point of view needs to involve the historical development of the whole of the human race."

This is a characteristic statement by Eichhorn, who was concerned to place all historical problems within a larger context and who basically was interested only in the development of the human intellectual and spiritual life. He ridiculed those pedants who failed to count the latest real problems as part of the study of history but rather wished to file them under "philosophy." The "history of philosophy" was for him an essential part of the study of history. His opponents were the three M.A. students at Halle: J. W. Rothstein, O. Ritschl, and J. Gloel.

The third of Eichhorn's theses merits particular attention: "New Testament introduction needs to be the history of early Christian literature." In general, one finds veiled particular or personal allusions lurking beneath the surface of the theses of doctoral candidates, and, in order to understand them, one needs to know at whom or at what notion in that particular discipline they are directed. Thus, Eichhorn's thesis that was just mentioned is to be taken as an attack on treating the New Testament in a purely literary-critical way and against a one-sided limiting of study to the New Testament canon. Eichhorn at times expressed the desire to issue an edition of the New Testament together with the apostolic fathers, so that people could see clearly that there is no absolute distinction, only a relative one, between the two bodies of writing.

It is not without merit to note that there is never any mention of "history of religion" or "the history of religion method" in any of the theses. Nevertheless, what Eichhorn is calling for here is basically that a history of religion approach be taken, even if such was not yet completely recognizable in his wording. [9] Ten year later Gustav Krüger[14] repeated Eichhorn's statement and provided a systematic justification for it; the aim of both writers was to include the books of the New Testament in a more comprehensive "early Christian literary history." However, Eichhorn's statement, or at least the idea that he had been the first to express concretely, had still further effects. In 1897 Wrede published a brief programmatic statement on the task and method of "so-called" New Testament theology[15] in which he called for the same to be done for New Testament theology as Eichhorn had demanded for New Testament introduction. At a later time, Wrede used these words to express the task:

> What is to be conveyed is not what individual writings and their authors say, but rather the task is to pay attention to the religious perspectives, sympathies and ideas themselves, ignoring the artificial boundaries drawn by the concept of the canon. The task is to elaborate, that is to clarify these ideas and to trace their course. In this sense I myself have … advocated the transformation of the conventional and, in my opinion, untenable discipline of New Testament theology into a history of early Christian religion and theology.[16]

It was Paul Wernle who next attempted to bring this program to fruition when he published *The Beginnings of Christianity*,[17] in which he ignored the boundaries of the canon. Thus we may understand and entirely agree with the approving judgment given by Harnack: "I do not believe I am in error when I claim that the gentle influence exercised by Eichhorn on the younger generation of church historians is of greater value than an entire course of lectures in the history of religion."[18]

One of Eichhorn's theses lets us see how steeped he was in Melanchthon's *Apology for the Augsburg Confession*. Number 17 says: "*Justificare* in the *Apology* means to make righteous," in stark contrast to the common

---

14. Gustav Krüger, *Das Dogma vom Neuen Testament* (Giessen: Münchow, 1896).

15. William Wrede, *Über Aufgabe und Methode der sogenannten Neutestamentlichen Theologie*, (Göttingen: Vandenhoeck & Ruprecht, 1897).

16. William Wrede, *Vorträge und Studien* (Tübingen: Mohr, 1907), 65–66.

17. Paul Wernle, *Die anfänge unserer religion* (Tübingen;: Mohr Siebeck, 1904), translated as *The Beginnings of Christianity* (trans. Gustav A. Bienemann; ed. with an introduction by William D. Morrison; 2 vols.; London: Williams & Norgate, 1903–1904). [Paul Wernle (1872–1939), Swiss Protestant New Testament theologian and church historian.]

18. Adolf von Harnack, *Reden und Aufsätze* (2nd corrected ed.; Tübingen: Mohr, 1904), 181–82.

belief that *justificare* in the evangelical sense always means "to declare righteous." A year later he wrote, still as a *Privatdozent*,[19] an essay that is dense and rather difficult to read, yet in many respects, particularly from the personal aspect, highly instructive: "Über die Rechtfertigungslehre der *Apologie*" ["On the Doctrine of Justification in the *Apology*"].[20] The first thing that catches the reader's attention is the critical strength of the piece; Eichhorn treats the problem in quite the opposite way to Loofs,[21] who had previously written on the topic in the same journal and to whom Eichhorn gladly acknowledges his indebtedness. [10] He is of the opinion that the reader sees only one side of the argument with Loofs, who has taken his lead from Ritschl, because important doctrines, especially the decisive concept of *promissio*, are ignored. On the other hand, Eichhorn goes in so little for polemics that it is possible to reconstruct only a rather imperfect idea of the views of his opponents from his discussion. Thus he does not limit himself to unfruitful refutation but rather tries to build a new and positive structure in order to display the *Apology* in all its power. This ability to penetrate to the heart of the matter was always a strength of Eichhorn's, and he spared no effort to remove the hindering outward layers of any material.

He has a sure hand right from the start in choosing the correct method, a method that needs to be different from that of the old dogmatic theologians. He does not answer the question about the meaning of justification in the time-honored "purely philological" fashion by examination and precise definition of the different concepts, because the expressions used by Melanchthon are not to be seen as technical terms. At the end of his treatise he presents in painstaking detail the proof that the *Apology* in fact lacks any clear terminology. Eichhorn's dislike of a one-sided privileging of the "philological method," although quickly reined in, shows through again in the first thesis of his doctoral dissertation:

---

19. [A *Privatdozent* (roughly, "private lecturer") has normally gained the *Habilitation*, been approved by a vote of the faculty, and is awaiting a call to a chair. *Privatdozenten* are expected to take part in the university system but may only be awarded a token salary and consequently have a rather problematic status, especially when one considers how much they must have achieved to get this far and the fact that they are at least approaching middle-age. The whole concept is under discussion at present in Germany.]

20. Albert Eichhorn, "Die Rechtfertigungslehre der *Apologie*," *TSK* 59 (1887): 415–91.

21. [Friedrich Loofs (1858–1928), Professor of Church History in Leipzig and Halle, was a pupil and friend of Harnack.]

"The etymology of *qādôš* is immaterial to the Old Testament concept of holiness."

Later he also developed an element of mistrust, as became noticeable in certain expressions he used. He showed great skill in castigating the weakness of the "philologists" and their return to the origins of language and consequent false deductions from etymology. He was equally cutting in his portrayal of their superstitious belief in the value of literary evidence and the way they heaped up irrelevant material; nevertheless, he freely conceded there was now a sea-change in the offing among the best of the philologists.

The chief purpose of his treatise was to bring out plainly how the life of faith proceeds, as it was described so precisely in the *Apologia*, by separating the clear and important statements from the peripheral and unclear ones. Thus he treats in order as the central articles: sin, law, repentance, the gospel, faith and its results. These doctrines, as he expounds them, are as simple as they are unambiguous, particularly because they also relate to each other.

Since these central concepts are established, the next thing is to give a firm and clear answer to the question of how justification is to be understood. [11] The prevailing view until that time had been that justification was to be understood in the forensic sense, because the famous paragraphs 125 and 183–186 were taken to be the *locus classicus*, and, based on this, the whole plan of the *Apologia* was laid out without more ado. But even Loofs had raised his voice against such a procedure. Eichhorn agrees with him and corroborates his evidence, especially by stressing that the conventional presentation is wrong because, if one follows its assumptions, justification bears no relation to the teaching of the gospel and of faith, whereas Melanchthon had set about to demonstrate precisely this connection.

> It is to sinners, whom the law condemns, who feel the wrath of God and the fear of death in their consciences, that the gospel proclaims God's promise, that he wishes to be merciful for Christ's sake, that he wishes to forgive all sins and take sinners to be his friends and heirs. Trusting in this divine promise sets their consciences free from all fear and brings them consolation and peace. We gain a trust and love for God, where we once fled from God as our judge. Because we love God, we can now fulfill the law, which is what this change of heart requires. Of course, such a fulfilling of the law remains imperfect, but we take consolation in the

grace of which we are certain through God's promise. This is what the *Apologia* means by justification. So justification is pardon or acceptance of sinners by God.[22]

As a result of this piece of work, in 1888 Eichhorn was called as an *ausserordentlicher Professor* in Halle.[23]

In the 1880s, as far as his health allowed, he undertook an intensive study of Migne's Patrologia graeca and showed himself possessed of almost unbounded capacity for initiatives in all areas of history. Together with this he absorbed the powerful impressions gained from personal contact with the broadest range of minds. Especially during the period when he was staying with Baumgarten, but also in the years that followed, to his great delight he joined company every Thursday for coffee with such a varied group of scholars as Rothstein, Otto Ritschl, Gloel (who died at a young age), Erich Schaeder, Karl Müller from Erlangen, of Reformed persuasion, P. von Koblinski, P. Winkelmann, and the hyperlutheran Martin von Gerlach.[24] Others joined the group later, such as Martin Schulze from Königsberg, Johann Ficker from Strasbourg,[25] G. Beelitz (Gunkel's father-in-law), and others. [12] All of them, including the systematic theologian Schaeder, whom he met again later in Kiel, maintained a personal attachment to the most radical one among them. At that time Baumgarten lived in the Händelstrasse, where Grafe and Loofs also kept their homes open to

---

22. Eichhorn, "Die Rechtfertigungslehre der *Apologie*," 416.

23. [This was traditionally the last stage before being named to a full tenured chair, where one had the title of *Ordinarius* or *Ordentlicher Professor*.]

24. [Johann Wilhelm Rothstein (1853–1926) was an Old Testament and Septuagint scholar. Otto Karl Albrecht Ritschl (1860–1944) was the eldest son of Albrecht Ritschl and a professor in Kiel and Bonn. Among other works, he wrote a biography of his father. He was perhaps best known for his four-volume history of Protestantism (*Dogmengeschichte des Protestantismus*, 1908–1927) and for his work on Nietzsche and Schleiermacher. Johannes Gloel (1857–1891) was a New Testament scholar. Erich Schaeder (1861–1936), systematic theologian and professor at Kiel, was principally concerned with developing a theocentric theology based on the Bible. Although his work helped prepare the way for Karl Barth's theological revolution, what he achieved has been largely forgotten. After a difficult start in the Lutheran-dominated context of Erlangen, Ernst Friedrich Karl Müller (1863–1935) eventually became Professor of Reformed Theology there in 1896. He excelled in the teaching of New Testament as well as systematic theology.]

25. [Johannes Ficker (1861–1944) was a theologian and archeologist who edited Luther's early lectures.]

Eichhorn. He valued highly his spirited relationship with Eduard Grafe,[26] in whose home he felt at greatest liberty to develop his talent for conversation, unhindered by the presence of other guests. Grafe was the friend who showed the greatest understanding for his ideas on the New Testament, and it was there that he also met with Jülicher, Karl Müller, and Troeltsch.[27] By nature compassionate, he drew strength from real introspection and from female company; this led him to make numerous visits to the house of Frau Thümmel, the wife of a senior official who acted as mother figure to the students.[28] The contact he was seeking was also provided by his tender-hearted landlady, Fräulein Herold, and later in Kiel by Fräulein Kraus; both ladies were of advanced age.

Eichhorn's scholarly influence in his years at Halle was important principally for many of the developing scholars, over whom he stood head and shoulders, not only by reason of his age, but by his knowledge and ability; they happily owned him as their spiritual head. The young scholars who gathered around him were very different individuals but united in their zeal for history. In the midst of the flow of their development, they were passionate about learning from each other and spurred each other on constantly around the meal table and on the frequent walks they took together. Members of the inner circle who felt a common bond, both intellectual and human, included Hermann Gunkel, who, in addition to his specialized knowledge of the Old Testament, added a wealth of other issues; Heinrich Zimmern, the Assyriologist with his firm grasp of Babylonian language and religion; and the Germanist Otto Bremer, with his mastery of the modern phonetic view of the language, at home in questions of rhythm, who, despite the remoteness of his discipline from those of the others, was of great value for his common interest in history.

But Eichhorn's influence reached beyond Halle to Göttingen, which he visited often and where he was constantly inspired and invigorated, par-

---

26. [Eduard Grafe (1855–1922) was Professor of New Testament in Kiel and Bonn.]

27. [Ernst Troeltsch (1865–1923), systematic theologian, philosopher, and sociologist of religion, was widely considered to be the most influential theologian of the history of religion school. He wrote numerous books, perhaps the most influential of which were *The Social Teaching of the Christian Churches* and *Protestantism and Progress: The Significance of Protestantism for the Rise of the Modern World*.]

28. [A *Studentenmutter* normally ran a boarding house or inn where students were welcome.]

ticularly through the agency of Wrede, so that "all of the *Privatdozenten* in Göttingen of those days were somehow touched by Eichhorn's spirit."[29]

As stimulating as his influence on the younger scholars was, nevertheless Eichhorn usually had great difficulty in capturing the interest of students, since he assumed too much knowledge, and, no doubt, the breadth of his vision made his lectures ramble. [13] Still, those who were qualified and interested were always to be found listening to him. His reputation reached as far as Leipzig, from where it drew older students who came not only on occasion but regularly to his public lectures, an hour in length, on "The History of the Main Theological Concepts" (sin, faith, the incarnation).

So, for example, in one particular semester there were four young people who met together. On each occasion one of the group used to make the journey across, write down carefully in note form or shorthand what was said, then report back to the others. Later, in Kiel, Eichhorn's relationship with the students remained the same. Erich Franz wrote in the *Schleswig-Holsteinisches Kirchenblatt* (14/26 [1913]):

> Those unforgettable lectures remain clearly imprinted in the memory— the feeling of deep and heartfelt gratitude, together with the awareness or the sense of the importance of this rare and outstanding scholar, with his outwardly unassuming air.... It must be admitted that his lectures, plain and unembellished as they were, but so full of stimulating thoughts, were often too hard for the students, especially the newer ones. You needed a certain level of academic maturity to follow them properly. This may to an extent excuse some who missed this opportunity, but it often seemed to me ironic when such splendid lectures sometimes attracted an audience of only half a dozen, or even fewer at certain talks. Of course the auditorium was packed at other times, so that a new venue had to be found. The public lectures were particularly impressive; it was Eichhorn's custom to give them alongside his main course on church history. It was nothing unusual for me to hear younger theologians talk about them with great enthusiasm.

Apart from the "History of the Main Theological Concepts" already mentioned, these public lectures included the "Account of the History of the Church" and the "History of the Enlightenment in the Seventeenth and Eighteenth Centuries." It is indicative of the material that interested him

---

29. Ernst Troeltsch (private communication to the author).

that shortly before his departure from the university he planned to prepare a new course of lectures on "The Cult of Devotion to the Saints and
Relics." He would fulfill a burning desire of his friends if now in the leisure of his retirement years he could bring himself to publish his studies
on the Enlightenment with the special treatment of contemporary sources
that he brought to the work.

If we wish to get a clear idea of what influenced him and the direction
his work took, we must emphasize in particular the finely trained historical sense that is his hallmark. [14] His bent toward history and historical
development is so striking that it has noticeably restricted the development of other skills. He takes a particular delight in allowing free rein to
this preference, so that metaphysical and dogmatic questions are ignored.
He shows as little interest in science as in philosophy; the beauty to be
found in both nature and art leave him cold. He visits no museums and
defines as beautiful those things that serve a practical purpose. When we
make such judgments we need to look between the lines and see the smile
on his face; you could do him no greater favor than to be indignant and
contradict him.

He loves to spend his leisure time playing chess but also plunges in
the mysteries of the world of numbers, taking great pleasure in calcula-
tions and complex problems, especially when he can tease and confound
his friends. Census statistics are a great passion, and every five years he
cannot rest until he has memorized the most important cities and their
population. He does have a good general knowledge but nothing extraordinary; in fact, he is proud of not being an "academic,"[30] and it is only in
retaining figures in his head that he takes real pleasure. Yet for the rest he
is a historian and has no desire to be anything else. But in this one discipline of history he is a person of infinite diversity who has managed to
attract at the same time the widest possible range of people and who has
mastered a vast array of issues even from areas far removed from theology. Just as the sense for history was so developed in himself, he sought
to encourage it in others so that they might perceive and portray only the
historical facts as they are, unaffected by dogma.

He himself only had one opportunity to show his skill as a historian
when in 1898 he wrote a monograph on *Das Abendmahl im Neuen Testa-*

---

30. [Gressmann makes an obscure play on Eichhorn's name when he adds: "here too
he is a real 'Eichhorn' "—the old form of *Eichhörnchen* (squirrel).]

ment [*The Lord's Supper in the New Testament*].[31] At the very outset he refutes the historical-critical method that is content to arrive at the earliest tradition through comparing the various texts and is thus convinced it has traced the historical development. Instead, he follows the "history of religion" method, which starts by dispensing with the text-critical variants and simply looks for the meaning of the traditions, which all clearly report the instigation of the communion in the church. So now the question is whether these reports are based on the reworking of an earlier tradition and why such a reworking should have occurred.

[15] A careful analysis shows that the words spoken at the Last Supper contain the explanation of Christ's death; this is a view that first prevailed in the Christian church. It was in the church that the powerful impulse won through, not only to solve the mystery of Christ's death, but to find the key to this mystery in the words of Jesus himself. Such a result is confirmed by the real, not symbolic, meaning of the Lord's Supper, where we partake supernaturally of the body and blood of Christ. In turn, this view can only be understood from the worship of the early church.

If we look more closely at the various versions of the episode, it is true that we catch a glimpse of some modification in the story, but it is impossible to ascertain with any certainty what the event originally meant in the context of Jesus' life: all conjectures are useless. Since in any case we cannot trace the concept of eating the body and drinking the blood of Christ back to Jesus himself, the problem arises of the origin of this sacramental idea in the early church. Obviously, supernatural eating and drinking was no cause for surprise among the first Christians, so sacramental meals must have been known to them. Thus Christ can be said to be the replacement for some other supernatural being. As Eichhorn decided at the time, it is not possible for the historian to get any closer to the matter, since we lack any external sources.

Eichhorn's book not only formulated the problem of history of religion precisely but also showed the right way forward for research on the Lord's Supper. Wilhelm Heitmüller[32] built further on the foundation laid by Eichhorn and advanced scholarly knowledge considerably by adduc-

---

31. [*Das Abendmahl im Neuen Testament* appeared as number 36 in the series Hefte zur "Christlichen Welt" and is included in translation in the present volume.]

32. In his book *Taufe und Abendmahl bei Paulus: Darstellung und religionsgeschichtliche Beleuchtung* (Göttingen: Vandenhoeck & Ruprecht, 1903) and in his article "Abendmahl" (*RGG* 1:20ff.). [Wilhelm Heitmüller (1869–1926) was Professor of New Tes-

ing a vast array of history of religion material and clearly explaining the underlying religious ideas by the use of parallels. Thus scholarship made progress in one area; however, Eichhorn's principal concern to discover the origin of the concept of the sacrament in the early church has received no clear response to this day, even though we may perhaps expect further clarification in the course of time.

There is also no progress to report on the other main question of what happened in the life of Jesus on "Maundy Thursday." In fact, we have taken a step backwards, for in this respect Eichhorn's bald refusal to show any interest in epistemology will reveal more to the uninitiated than the finest conjectures that conceal our ignorance and make the problem less pressing.

[16] In the process, Eichhorn posed the following question to New Testament scholars: "We need to ask which material has been transformed by the faith of the church and what were the underlying motives in play as this occurred. Then we will discover that the transformation went deeper than scholars normally assume. We will also find that this process was not a uniform one in every place."[33] Eichhorn himself only alluded to the particular question of how the historical tradition about Jesus was altered by the notion that Jesus knew in advance and predicted his death and resurrection. Wrede singled out and confirmed this point, placing it in a wider context as he gave full weight to Eichhorn's principles. Thus at first he considered the idea of Jesus' messiahship to be a mere conjecture made by the early church, but then he did further research on its development and what basis it might have in the historical Jesus. Nor did this exhaust Eichhorn's agenda. He himself points to the far-reaching transformation undergone by everything "that has to do with death and resurrection. The birth narrative was likewise reconstructed." Apart from some occasional observations, the problems of the resurrection and birth legends have still not been thoroughly researched in the sense of the "history of religion" approach; in fact, they have been given scarcely any serious attention.

Eichhorn's little treatise is of great interest and to be recommended as a model not only for its content but for its methodology. He emphasizes repeatedly that his observations are from a "history of religion" point

---

tament in Marburg, Bonn, and Tübingen. With Ernst Troeltsch, Johannes Weiss, and Paul Wernle, he is considered one of the main theologians of the history of religion school.]

33. See *The Lord's Supper in the New Testament*, 75 below.

of view, which "in the current climate … are not yet considered to be of scholarly validity."[34] This is where we first find the term "history of religion" in Eichhorn's work. The term is not to be taken to mean, as often occurs these days, that non-Christian religions are imported into the equation, since it is only at the end that these are mentioned obliquely. Eichhorn does not use any analogies from other religions at all: all his researches without exception hinge on early Christian traditions. The emphasis that he wants to make is on the word *history*, more specifically on the *history of the biblical religion*. Well, what is new about that? Has this not been the goal of previous scholars too? [17] Of course, but they followed different paths to attain their goal. In the case at hand, the "history of religion" is used in contrast to literary criticism. Now of course all research is dependent on the texts and is thus unable to do without textual criticism. It is only the exclusive use of the latter that Eichhorn opposes: literal critical scrutiny alone cannot shed light on the growth and development of a religion. For that it needs a different way of posing questions.

Those wishing to get a picture of the history of a religion must not be satisfied with researching the history of its texts; they must go further and study the history of the material and the ideas. It is certainly essential to follow the changes that occurred in the texts and, particularly in the case of the Lord's Supper, to pay heed to the variant readings; however, texts change only under the influence of new ideas. Thus one can see the development of the religion itself mirrored in the variant readings, and it is only when one has reconstructed this development that it is really possible to offer an explanation for the changes in the form of the words as they are handed down. Demonstrating how these internal forces work means quite simply taking the concept of history with absolute seriousness.

Now the first basic rule is to deduce the development of a religion from its own motives. Eichhorn agrees with this, and he too continues the attempt—which was put into motion before his time—to trace the idea of the sacrament that is indisputably found in Paul back to Jesus himself. But this is where the fundamental difference between Eichhorn and his predecessors comes in, for what seemed possible to them is for him impossible. He can find no way to bridge across from Jesus to Paul; he finds instead a great gulf fixed between the two. This astonishing result, whether true or not, may be explained as stemming from a refinement of the historical

---

34. Ibid., 87.

sense. Eichhorn is careful not to read into the words of Jesus something that is not there. The modern aversion to magic had caused the earlier scholars to unwittingly reject the statements about the Lord's Supper in the Synoptic Gospels and to reinterpret them as having some other sense, usually an allegorical one.

In contrast to this approach, Eichhorn strenuously emphasizes the bald fact—no matter how uncomfortable it may be to the modern mind, no matter how badly it fits with our concept of Jesus—that even the Synoptic writers are only acquainted with the sacramental interpretation of the Lord's Supper. Nowadays it is scarcely possible to credit how this could have been misunderstood, but at that time it was a real discovery! It was only possible to accept it as a fact because Eichhorn's interests were exclusively historical ones and because he did not allow himself to be blinkered by either dogmatic or antidogmatic preconceptions. [18] The second factor to be added to the sharpening of the focus of historical conscience is a more profound psychological interpretation. No matter how Jesus conceived of the Lord's Supper, no one can invent a way to make credible the notion that the sacramental meal was spontaneously generated in the early church. The idea of eating the body and drinking the blood of a divine being, an idea that is so hard for our sensibilities to accept, could only have been promulgated if it linked in with something else and if Christ replaced some other major supernatural entity. Since Judaism knows nothing of sacramental meals we must at this point postulate the influence of some different religion. So Eichhorn refuses out of principle to attempt to trace the sacramental act of breaking of bread to any supposed "psychological method" that might stem from some original kind of "symbolic" act—an attempt that used to be made and is still current. Such a construction would make a mockery of real psychological insights.

What he does discover here is a rupture in early Christianity's organic development, and it is this gap that in his opinion provides an entry for a different religion. It is not psychology but its misuse that he rejects. He does not attack the attempt to explain a religion by reference to itself; what he is against is extending this principle too far at the cost of historical verisimilitude.

There is also a personal trait observable in Eichhorn's treatise, and the secret of his fertile genius is based on this trait, although of course only to a certain point. Page 12 [72 below] of the work is full of quotations from the Bible that play a decisive role in the evidence he is adducing. What we are interested in here is not the content but the distinctive psychological characteristics of the author. He is hoping to make a specific impression on his readers, whom he imagines to think similarly to himself. Just as he needs to be presented with a sensory image in order to make a clear judgment about an issue, he presumes the same to be true of others, although this ability is precisely what "scholars" often lack. Because he wants to see, and if possible perceive something with all his senses, he immerses himself in it until he has gained a vivid image and can describe it in all its detail. Such a determination not only brings him clarity and precision of thought, but it spurs him on to more and more new questions and issues.

He draws analogies to shed light on a situation, or he makes comparisons to illustrate an idea. [19] He particularly loves to bring out contrasts and differences. What he is doing is something like the way πίστις in the early church meant recognizing a symbol, whereas *fides* in the Middle Ages meant being convinced of revealed truth and *faith* for the Reformers meant trust in God's promise. Or, turning his spotlight on the history of popular education, he might compare the tracking down of witches under Charlemagne in order to give them a friendly warning with the same procedure at the end of the Middle Ages, but with the different purpose of burning them. Eichhorn had this effect on all those who allowed themselves to be influenced by him: he demanded they take a three-dimensional view and paint a vivid, colorful canvas, just as he did, painstaking in attention to detail, in order to bring to life the period being studied. Where material is lacking because the tradition is only piecemeal, he requires them to at least ask the questions and plot the limits of what is known.

True though it is to speak of Eichhorn's great powers of imagination, it is equally true to speak of his great lack in the area of systematic thought. His favorite philosopher was Lotze, whose work *Mikrokosmus* he knew intimately.[35] This predilection was shared by the religious his-

---

35. [Hermann Rudolf Lotze (1817–1881) wrote *Mikrokosmus; Ideen zur Naturgeschichte und Geschichte der Menschheit; Versuch einer Anthropologie* (3 vols.; Leipzig: Hirzel, 1856–1864), translated as *Microcosmus: An Essay concerning Man and His Relation to the World* (trans. Elizabeth Hamilton and E. E. Constance Jones; New York: Scribner & Welford, 1885). The philosophy of Lotze is called "spiritualistic monism," a type of idealistic monistic philosophy that makes thought the essential factor in philosophy. He was influ-

torian Edward Lehmann.[36] Even his exchanges with his friend Külpe could be better classified as experimental psychology than as philosophical systematics. No doubt this marks a limit to his abilities, even if the free development of his latent powers was curtailed by the nervous disorder he suffered at the end of the 1880s, no doubt as the result of overwork, leaving him thereafter very few hours in the day in which he could work. At any rate, it is typical of the man that he never coalesced his individual historical observations. It is in the brief overview that his work has its life; his thoughts take the form of endless separate remarks strung together haphazardly in conversation. Bubbling over with ideas independent of each other, with cleverly phrased questions, even with paradoxical thoughts, he is one of those intriguing people who exude a charismatic influence. You never leave his company without having been enriched inwardly and one way or another filled with an inspiration that has totally unpredictable consequences. He loves to hear the views of others expounded, but he would rather contradict than agree. Criticism is his gift, an ever-productive one, almost always hitting the nail on the head and usually going quite a deal further, so that people happily submit to it, no matter how pointed it may be, knowing that Eichhorn himself is quite ready to accept being challenged in his turn.

[20] One might compare him with Plato's Socrates among the sophists. Like Socrates he made his mark by his conversations, not his writings, and mesmerized those around him by his insight. Quoting no authorities, casting his eye neither left nor right, he goes straight to the problem, bringing others to admit their ignorance, or else he spurs them on to their own discoveries. We may even venture to say that he served as a midwife not only to many individuals in their scholarship but to the whole history of religion movement by his faithful advice to each one of them.

His countless remarks are always witty, honed to the point, full of insight and import, often illuminating the whole picture in a flash, and if some friend or even Eichhorn himself were to compile them, what a treasure for German scholarship that would be! But born in an instant, they are swallowed up in an instant. Yet their effect remains.

---

enced by Alexander von Humboldt's *Kosmos* and Herder's *Ideen zu einer Geschichte der Menschheit*.]

36. [Edward Lehmann (1862–1930) was co-author of a number of textbooks on church history.]

In 1889 Hermann Gunkel came to Halle. His father and grandfather had spurred him on to study religion, history, and literature, casting him for life in that mould. Even while a schoolboy he was captivated by Gustav Freytag's pictures from Germany's past and by the notes on Scheffel's *Ekkehard*.[37] Among his theological teachers, Harnack, Stade,[38] Ritschl, and Lagarde exercised the most marked influence on him. His development ran parallel to that of Eichhorn and Wrede in many respects. He too was from Hanover, from the Lutheran State Church; he too had been a student of Ritschl's. On the other hand, he was six years younger than Eichhorn and was influenced by Harnack and Wellhausen, so that you might say he belonged almost to a younger generation. As a student he had started to make independent attempts to account for the New Testament, convinced as he was that enlightenment was to be found in its immediate predecessors, not in the Old Testament. To this end he engaged in the study of the Apocrypha and for a time believed he had discovered in the apocalyptic literature what should be acknowledged as that prior stage. At the same time he cast around in the setting of Judaism with the prior conviction that no people or religion can be understood without its context. In addition, in Göttingen he worked through the Egyptian monuments of Lepsius,[39] bent on improving our knowledge of the Old Testament.

Young scholars of that period were experiencing a new wave of enthusiasm for history breaking over them; feeling inhibited by the barriers of the canon, they realized they needed to lift their eyes and take in the whole picture. [21] With this as his grounding, Gunkel came to Halle and there, as previously in Göttingen, was knit in friendship with Eichhorn. For a time he conferred with his older, more experienced and mature friend, who was no expert on the Old Testament, placing the scholarly content of each of his lecture series before him, describing the issues and outlining

---

37. [Joseph Viktor von Scheffel (1826–1886) wrote *Ekkehard: Eine Geschichte aus dem zehnten Jahrhundert* (Philadelphia: Morwitz, 1855), a historical novel set in the tenth century that includes 279 notes citing references to sources. It was published in English as *Ekkehard: A Tale of the Tenth Century* (trans. Sofie Delffs; Leipzig: Tauchnitz, 1872).]

38. [Bernhard Stade (1848–1906), became Professor of Old Testament at Giessen. He wrote a critical history of Israel (*Geschichte des Volks Israel*, 2 vols., 1887–1888) and several Hebrew lexical and grammatical works, as well as a biblical theology of the Old Testament.]

39. [The Egyptologist Karl Richard Lepsius (1810–1884) published the monumental work *Denkmäler aus Ägypten und Äthiopien* (12 vols.; Berlin: Nicolaische Buchhandlung, 1849–1856).]

the pros and cons. It then became Eichhorn's task to offer a critique and give advice on the basis of what he had been told. In this period of fermenting and developing his mature approach, Eichhorn's judgment was of inestimable worth, especially as he [Gunkel] commenced his preliminary studies for *Schöpfung und Chaos*[40] and had the pleasure of being an intimate in the circle of friends at Halle.

But soon after that, the tragedy of Eichhorn's illness struck, forcing him to take repeated long periods of leave and to quit Halle. During Eichhorn's absence, Gunkel was writing his book and used to read him sections of it whenever he came back. Gunkel took no greater delight in anything than in his approval. When it appeared in 1895, it was dedicated "To Albert Eichhorn in friendship and with gratitude," and in the foreword we read:

> The author is particularly grateful to the one whose name appears in the dedication. Years ago, it was his support that affirmed me in principles and in research methods when my conscience was beset by unexpected opposition [Gunkel is referring to the difficulties he experienced with the theological faculty at Halle after his *Habilitation*]. Drawing from the deep well of his probing and his responses helped me sharpen my senses. It was my frequent custom to share with him the results of the present work as soon as I had established them; his counsel, approval and dissent have all been of equal worth to me in my project. (vii)

In 1901 Eichhorn gave his position over to Voigt and moved to Kiel, where he functioned as an *ausserordentlicher Professor*[41] until the end of his academic career in 1913, poor in public recognition and honors but enriched by the appreciation and respect of those whose privilege it was to know him more fully. He took even more pleasure, if that were possible, in his contact with those of other faculties than with his closer associates. I too may count myself one of those friends and owe him a lifelong debt of gratitude not only for the way he assisted in the advancement of my scholarly education but also for his caring involvement in my life. I dedicated

---

40. Hermann Gunkel, *Schöpfung und Chaos: Eine religionsgeschichtliche Untersuchung über Gen. 1 und Ap. Joh. 12* (Göttingen: Vandenhoeck & Ruprecht, 1895), translated most recently as *Creation and Chaos in the Primeval Era and the Eschaton: A Religio-historical Study of Genesis 1 and Revelation 12* (trans. K. William Whitney Jr.; Grand Rapids: Eerdmans, 2006).

41. [The closest American equivalent would be adjunct professor.]

my book on the origin of Israelite Jewish eschatology[42] to him as a δόσις ὀλιγή τε φιλή τε.[43] [22] His name only rarely receives a mention there, much less often than I would have liked, but in typically modest fashion he never sets great store by being quoted. I could have mentioned him on every page, even though it was hard to distinguish in each case exactly what his contribution had been—from start to finish he discussed every problem with me. I presented him with the material that lay outside his expertise, together with my opinion, in order to hear what he thought.

He had the extraordinary ability, one that I have never experienced with anyone else, of grasping even the most long-winded hypotheses as soon as you uttered them, of picking out their weak point, and of mercilessly and inexorably dismantling every house of cards you set up, until it was impossible to rebuild. More often than not he then quickly erected his own version over against the demolished one. I admit his new position could rarely be pressed into service in the form that he had so deftly given it. By their very nature his flashes of insight had to be confirmed by dint of hard slog with factual evidence. This of course meant that changes were likely. But this is how you learn to practice self-discipline and let no claim stand without a thorough basis. There was no instance of "cheating"—to use his striking term—that could escape his eye, if you had perhaps been trying to "adapt" the tradition to fit a favorite theory.

True, he was an incorruptible judge who fairly weighed up the evidence for and against, but on the other hand he was ever willing to admit there could be different views. In fact, he went so far as to encourage you to continue to disagree. Nevertheless, he always insisted on drawing a clear distinction between the assured results of scholarship and a hypothesis. In the foreword I hint at the contribution he made to the book:

> I have greatly valued my personal contact with Professor Eichhorn, whose clear eye and sober judgment have so often served as a stimulus to me. His sincere interest and genuine pleasure in their successes prompts others to do their own independent research and strengthens their feeling of independence.

---

42. [Hugo Gressmann, *Der Ursprung der israelitisch-judischen Eschatologie* (Göttingen: Vandenhoeck & Ruprecht, 1905).]

43. ["A small but welcome gift" (Homer, *Odyssey* 6.208 and 14.58).]

Eichhorn was also a collaborator in the encyclopedic dictionary *Die Religion in Geschichte und Gegenwart*. As Baumgarten says at the end of his article on "Aberglaube" ["Superstition"], he is grateful to Eichhorn for numerous suggestions made in private conversation. Eichhorn himself contributed only one essay that bears his name: "Sacred History,"[44] which starts by clarifying the distinction between Catholicism and Protestantism in that regard. [23] For the former, sacred history was not finished with the closure of the canon. Rather, the Catholic Church continues it through all of history up to the present, all the time accompanied by miracles, revelations, and the saints. Catholicism finds its freedom of movement only minimally restricted by the Bible: to the Church, the classical period is the medieval, not the apostolic, age.

Protestantism, on the other hand, has made a fundamental break with the supernatural nature of church history, thus freeing religion from the burden of the past. From now on, the same principles apply to church history that apply to history in general. Conversely, the Bible was viewed in the same way; in fact, there was an increase in its absolute importance, since the sacred history of the Bible was now fundamentally distinct from all other human development. Modern theology then underwent a new revolution that treated first the Old, then the New Testament as "profane" and gradually subjected them completely to secular scholarship. From now on it is impossible to distinguish outwardly between sacred history and everything else that happens in the world. "The wellspring of religion lies within the religious person, and the people of God in the Old and New Testament take their turn in being part of it." Of course the special, sacred nature of the Bible has pressed its claim throughout Protestantism to this very day. Eichhorn finds an illustration of this continuing power in the constant demand for a return to a "biblical basis" and for a "theology of the facts of salvation."[45]

Thus though it is true to say that Eichhorn himself wrote little, this modest body of work was of great and lasting effect. In addition to his writings, three books were dedicated to him, and they will sound his

---

44. [Albert Eichhorn, "Heilige Geschichte," in *Die Religion in Geschichte und Geg-enwart* (ed. Friedrich Michael Schiele and Leopold Zscharnack; 5 vols.; Tübingen: Mohr Siebeck, 1909–13), 2:2023–27. A translation of this article is included as an appendix in the present volume.]

45. [For the significance of these terms and Eichhorn's attitude toward them, see section 4 of the appendix.]

praises as long as they find readers. Rade[46] once jokingly posed this awkward question: What might future scholars conclude if after some two thousand years the libraries of the Germany of today are dug up out of the rubble of the centuries and they discover that so many books are dedicated to one man—and virtually nothing is found that was written by that man? The myth of this figure will only be given more credibility and talk of this great scholar whose mighty works—now lost for all time—once reigned supreme over historical theology in Germany. In fact, they would not be completely wrong: no one else could have written them or will ever write them. [24] But enough of speculation: Eichhorn has already become a legend, something he bears with good grace and humor. In Wilhem Rauschenbusch's *Christianizing the Social Order*, we find the following statement:

> One of the most fruitful intellectual movements in Germany (the so-called *religionsgeschichtliche Schule*) owes its beginning to one man, Professor Albert Eichhorn. His health has been so frail that he has published nothing but a sixteen-page pamphlet, but by personal conversations he inspired a number of able young minds, setting them new problems and fertilizing their thinking by his unselfish cooperation.[47]

Here Eichhorn serves along with others as an example of the significance of individual men in history.

In the meantime, the love of truth that he personifies demands a small but not insignificant correction. Eichhorn was not *the* founder but *one* of the founders of the history of religion school and shares that responsibility with others. His contribution is more indirect and thus not easy to encapsulate in detail: by his personal influence he was for many of their representatives the critic and "selfless adviser," as we read in the citation for the honorary doctorate he was awarded by the Giessen theological faculty in 1908.

---

46. [See note 55 below.]

47. [Walter Rauschenbusch (1861–1918) was an American Baptist minister who is called "the father of the social gospel." He believed in societal reform rather than individual Christianity. His aim was to make earth more like a heavenly ideal rather than promoting personal salvation through Christ's particular atonement, a doctrine he rejected. His book *Christianizing the Social Order* was published by Macmillan in New York in 1912; the quotation is from pages 460–61.]

If the history of religion school, apart from certain of its branches, managed by and large to remain shielded from major *faux pas*, this virtue too may be traced back essentially to Eichhorn. Like a sower who is not allowed to participate in the harvest, he was prodigal in casting his seed where it would bring him no advantage on the wide field of knowledge. He had the delight of seeing the seed grow and bring forth abundant fruit. "His trench became a river and his river an ocean." This may be said as today's result of the work he accomplished in more than twenty-five years as an *ausserordentlicher Professor*, and it is our hope that we shall continue to learn from him in years to come and draw new strength from the stimulus he provides. All Eichhorn's friends—and here I am borrowing words of Gunkel's that apply to others as well—consider themselves to have been most privileged to have known him. They value him not only for his intellectual abilities but also because of his unimpeachable character as a man of such remarkable kindness that no mean thought has ever crossed his mind. He is generous to those who disagree with him, gentle to all those who suffer and are misunderstood, considerate to children and courteous to women. He carries their best wishes at all times and they ask that he will remain mindful of his faithful friends and students.

2. THE HISTORY OF RELIGION SCHOOL

It is not possible to mention Eichhorn's name without thinking of the *religionsgeschichtliche Schule*—the history of religion school.[48] But this is a catchword that, like all catchwords, is to be taken with a grain of salt and is only half true. First, it may be objected that such a "school" in the strict sense of the word does not exist at all, because it has no founder and because in addition there is no coherent entity—not even a loose unity—among its adherents.

It is appropriate to speak of a "Wellhausen school" or an "Usener[49] school," although even here the term does not completely fit and must not be pressed in the individual cases. All such terminology arises from the desire to put a convenient label on a particular scholar and thus categorize him as one entry in a group of similar scholars. Such classification is often most unfair, doing violence as it does to the individuality of each person. Nevertheless, it has the advantage of simplifying the wide range of expres-

---

48. [The German title *die religionsgeschichtliche Schule* has been rendered into English in various ways over the years. In the English translation of Ernst Troeltsch's fine article, "The Dogmatics of the 'Religionsgeschichtliche Schule,'" *AJT* (17 [1913]: 1–21), it is observed that the closest term in English (at that time) was "comparative religion," but the editors have added a note: "It has seemed best in this article to retain the German word rather than to employ an unsatisfactory circumlocution" (1 n. 1). Some have translated it "history of religions school," but this is subject to the objection that the main advocates of the method did not always like the word "school" (see below; Troeltsch also gives his reasons for avoiding this term ["The Dogmatics of the 'Religionsgeschichtliche Schule,'" 3]), nor, indeed, did translators always think that "religions" in the plural was an appropriate rendering, as it drew attention away from the broad concept of "religion" that the founders had in mind and splintered it into its various representative manifestations. For a summary of this argument and its history, see Eric J. Sharpe, "The Study of Religion in the *Encyclopedia of Religion*" (*JR* 70 [1990]: 340–52, esp. 345).]

49. [Hermann Carl Usener (1834–1905) was a classical philologist and philosopher of religion.]

sions that any academic area may assume, of allowing a clearer overview and of summarizing the common features of a great range of scholars.

So the word "school," if it is to have any meaning at all, is generally to be understood as describing a group of academics who essentially take a similar approach and come from pretty much the same position, ask related questions and by and large have the same basic view of things.

But there is a second, more important objection to the term. No doubt it is possible to claim with justification that the history of religion was pursued as an activity before the history of religion school and that such study is not neglected by scholars who do not belong to this school. So, according to this view, the term is subject to criticism for giving the impression that the history of religion school has the monopoly on the history of religion. Now the school in question has no intention of making any such claim. Like any academic development, it stands on the shoulders of the generations that have preceded it and has a thousand threads that link it to the past. [26] It is well aware of this whole context and gratefully acknowledges the filial obligation of sons who, without their fathers, would not be what they are. The history of religion school is happy to honor two men above all others as its spiritual forebears: Julius Wellhausen and Adolf Harnack.[50] Now both of these men regard the members of the history of religion school as their ill-bred sons, but they cannot deny their paternity. Nor should the fathers lament the fact that their sons show a different spirit from their own, for that is the way of the world, even in scholarship. It would be untrue to pretend that the history of religion school is something brand new. However, if we wish to emphasize what is original about their contribution, we should not concentrate so much on the common links but on what separates them. We need to highlight the contrast between them and the "schools" of both past and present that most closely resemble them. What is distinctive is not *the fact* that they practice the history of religion but *how* they practice it.

---

50. [Adolf (von) Harnack (1851–1930) was a major advocate of the historical-critical approach as a means of understanding the development of Christianity. He believed that a metaphysical approach could not get at the essential Christian history and thus that later church dogma had obscured Christ's message. He wrote copiously. Among his most important works are a series of popular lectures entitled *Das Wesen des Christentum*, published in 1900 (*What Is Christianity?* or *The Essence of Christianity*) and his earlier multivolume *Lehrbuch der Dogmengeschichte* (1894–1898; *A History of Dogma*).]

We cannot a priori answer the question of what is particular about the history of religion school by examining the term itself, since as a term it is far too neutral and can thus be interpreted in various ways. The question can only be addressed a posteriori from the facts of history. The movement known under this name began simultaneously in the areas of Old and New Testament study with the two books by Hermann Gunkel (*Schöpfung und Chaos*[51]) and Wilhelm Bousset (*Der Antichrist in der Überlieferung des Judentums, des Neuen Testaments und der alten Kirche*[52]), both appearing in 1895. Hardly a generation had passed since the publication of the first part of Julius Wellhausen's groundbreaking history of Israel, later known as the *Prolegomena zur Geschichte Israels.*[53] If we seem to be emphasizing these two dates, 1878 and 1895, we are doing so in the spirit of Eichhorn, who enjoyed adding general comments such as how much faster scholarly views change in the present than they used to in days gone by. Nevertheless, we must not forget that even now the history of religion school has still not entirely won the day. Its greatest victories have been in the area of New Testament studies, where it has found no worthy opponents and where consequently scholarly endeavor is undergoing a decisive influence because of this school.

[27] On the other hand, the history of religion school has encountered the stiffest resistance in the disciplines of Old Testament and church history, because here they had to overcome the more or less clearly expressed opposition of the two dominant authorities, Wellhausen in Old Testament and Harnack in church history. In the meantime Wellhausen has retreated from contention and Harnack has shown himself rather better disposed

---

51. [See above, note 40.]

52. Göttingen: Vandenhoeck & Ruprecht, 1895, translated as *The Antichrist Legend: A Chapter in Christian and Jewish Folklore* [trans. with a prologue on the Babylonian dragon myth by A. H. Keane; London: Hutchinson, 1896]). [Wilhelm Bousset (1865–1920) was regarded with suspicion by many more conservative thinkers because of his leading role in the history of religion movement. Although given very little official recognition during his lifetime, he contributed by his presence in Göttingen to that city's growing reputation for biblical scholarship, even as a *Privatdozent* (see above, note 18) and later as an *außerordentlicher Professor für Neues Testament* (adjunct, nontenured professor; at first with an annual income of only 1,800 marks).]

53. Julius Wellhausen, *Prolegomena zur Geschichte Israels* (Berlin: Reimer, 1878), translated as *Prolegomena to the History of Israel with a Reprint of the Article Israel from the "Encyclopaedia Britannica"* (trans. J. Sutherland Black and Allan Menzies; preface by W. Robertson Smith; Edinburgh: Black, 1885).

toward the young movement. After all, it is no doubt thanks largely to him that a chair of religion has been established in Berlin. Nevertheless, he still raises a note of warning, for which we are grateful.

Of more consequence is the continuing reality that scholars in the history of religion are prevented from occupying chairs of theology in Prussia. The instigators of this policy seem not to ask themselves whether they are perhaps doing irreparable damage to the progress of theological knowledge. It is not possible for them to stem a natural and ineluctable development. As well as Gunkel and Bousset, there are other leaders of the movement, such as Eichhorn and Wrede, Wernle and Heitmüller, Troeltsch, Pfleiderer,[54] and Baumgarten, who, each in his own way and through his own discipline, have advanced the research project of the history of religion school far beyond biblical exegesis and church history, into the realms of systematic and practical theology.

Innumerable friends and students have joined their number, and, if one hoped to count them, one would have to provide an overview of the latest Protestant scholarship.[55] The days do not seem far off when the history of religion school will have imparted something of its spirit to scholarship as a whole. One encouraging sign of how far the ideas of these scholars have spread in the last decade is the fact that even those from the right wing of the church can no longer completely avoid the history of religion viewpoint; we need mention only Sellin in this regard.[56]

The almost unparalleled success enjoyed by the history of religion school, despite the opposition of individual church authorities and faculties as well as state authorities, can only be explained by the fact that times were favorable in general. Study of religion may be described as the most popular study of our day, having grown not only from a biblical base but also from orientalist, classical, and Germanic foundations. [28] There are various causes for the heightened interest that is now directed

---

54. [Johann Gottlob Pfleiderer (1825–1897) was influential in educating children in the pietist/Methodist tradition and an advocate of the Methodist Holiness movement in Germany.]

55. As Rade has done in his comprehensive article "Religionsgeschichte und religionsgeschichtliche Schule" (*RGG* 4:2183–2200). [Paul Martin Rade (1857–1940) was a theologian and politician and founder of the journal *Die Christliche Welt* in 1886 and its editor until 1931. From Marburg, he founded a corresponding movement to that of Rauschenbusch (see above, note 45): the Christian social conferences.]

56. [Ernst Franz Max Sellin (1867–1946) was an Old Testament scholar and archeologist.]

in almost every quarter toward this study. It is partly brought about by the new discoveries that have recently been made during numerous excavations and expeditions, especially in the Near East. In part it has come about as the result of advances in the realm of philology, bringing together ancient and modern documents in the history of religion from near and far and subjecting them to historical study. Finally, it is in part due to the recent dramatic increase in appreciation of religious issues and of religion itself. The investigation of the development of these questions had been unreasonably neglected for a long time. However, the decisive element is the growing refinement of the historical sense that is also beneficial for the history of religion. Hegel's philosophy of religion, which fitted well with the speculative interests of a previous generation, also significantly advanced the study of other religions, as Reischle rightly stresses.[57] However, it is the present generation that is characterized by the specifically historical direction of study.

So the appearance of the history of religion school in the field of theology is only a token of a broader overall movement making its mark in all areas of knowledge. But it is to the credit of just a few that they have recognized this spirit of the times and quite consciously laid claim to the history of religion approach for the study of theology as well. Foremost among these is Paul de Lagarde,[58] who insisted in 1873 that theology in principle be turned into the study of religion.[59] However, he was a lone voice crying in the wilderness; although prophetically he showed the way to the following generation, he himself never managed to go beyond general statements on the topic. It was to be Bousset and Gunkel who were the first, in 1895, to apply the principle in practice to individual materials and thus assist it to gain a powerful momentum. Eichhorn and Zimmern backed Gunkel up in this.

---

57. Max Wilhelm Theodor Reischle, *Theologie und Religionsgeschichte* (Tübingen: Mohr Siebeck, 1904), 13. [Reischle (1858–1905) was Professor of Practical Theology in Giessen, then of Systematic Theology in Göttingen and later in Halle.]

58. [Paul Anton de Lagarde (1827–1891), Professor of Near Eastern Languages in Göttingen from 1869, worked on the Septuagint and on editions of the Bible and church fathers in Aramaic, Coptic, Syriac, Arabic, Greek, and Latin. He strove for the separation of church and state, but also a national church.]

59. He repeated this demand in *Deutsche Schriften* (repr.; Göttingen: Dieterich, 1903), 67ff. [The Nazi party later made use of his view, expressed in the *Deutsche Schriften*, that the presence of Jews was a hindrance to the unification of Germany.]

Thus the history of religion school, despite having emerged independently with its own particular characteristics, has a close affinity with the study of religion in general and with Near Eastern and classical studies of religion in particular. It is to be distinguished most clearly in particular from two schools that are related to each other: panbabylonianism[60] and comparative mythology. [29] On the other hand, despite certain differences and even disparities, it is almost possible to speak of a community of interest between the history of religion school and the "Usener school": I refer to the area of Hellenistic religion, in which context we need only to mention the names of Reitzenstein, Wendland, and Norden.[61]

It is hard to give any unified view of a phenomenon presenting so many and varied faces as the one known under the heading "history of religion school." So, for example, first one, then another feature has been highlighted.[62] The emphasis has been placed on "religion" in contrast to dogma and church and on "religion" with respect to the personal piety of individuals, especially the outstanding ones. It is true, to be sure, that this is the greatest, the ultimate task of all historical research in the field of religion. But there has never been any argument on that point, and even if the task is far from being complete and needs continual revitalization, the adherents of the history of religion school can join hands with their opponents in the knowledge that they are at one in this endeavor. Where the disagreements begin is with the question of how best to realize this common theological ideal.

At present, there is popular support for the view that the history of religion school is trying above all to bring other religions to a closer understanding of Judaism and Christianity. But even this view does not get to the heart of the movement, although at a superficial level it might seem reasonable. Well before the advent of the history of religion school, astute theologians, in particular the Rationalists, were alert to analogies

---

60. [Panbabylonianism was the theory that the astral element in a variety of religions showed they had a common origin, and this origin was in Babylon. An article that gives a good impression of the issue in the period when Gressmann was writing is Crawford H. Toy, "Panbabylonianism," *HTR* 3 (1910): 47–84.]

61. [Richard August Reitzenstein (1861–1931) was a Protestant scholar of classical and biblical languages, as was Johann Theodor Paul Wendland (1864–1915). Eduard Norden (1868–1941) was likewise a Protestant scholar of classical and biblical languages and a historian of religion.]

62. For more details, see Carl Clemen, *Die religionsgeschichtliche Methode in der Theologie* (Giessen: Ricker, 1904), 2ff.

and parallels in other religions. Indeed, they often came to the conclusion that these were influences on Christianity. But this was done mostly on the basis of dogmatic points of view that are rejected by modern historians of religion, who concentrate only on the historical development. It is no doubt true to say that all scholars today find themselves in agreement with the history of religion school that it is generally necessary to take into account the influence of other religions on Judaism and Christianity. It is in the realm of the individual views that the battle flares up.

Now it would look very bad for the importance of the history of religion school to theological study if it concentrated on nothing more than the effects of other religions on Christianity. But it has never done that, nor will it ever do so. [30] For theologians, studying the history of religion means above all studying the history of their own religion. Any other stance is excluded from the outset.[63] Of course, this was also the wish of earlier generation; in fact, it may be claimed that this is an obvious goal for anyone who has in any way learned to think historically. On the other hand, there is great variation in the methods adopted. We have seen the emergence of new questions and ways of viewing the issues, and they promise to do a better job of helping us reach our goal. So the research methods of the current generation are markedly different from those of their predecessors.

In addition, theology can only very slowly extricate itself from the supernatural bonds that have ensnared it for over a thousand years. It has not been until our own times, free as they are in every respect from dogma and concerned to hold neither a dogmatic nor an antidogmatic position, that we have been able to do justice to the concept of history, now that psychological methods of historical study are being more and more refined. A few examples may shed light on the individual details of this progress without any necessity first to take into account the effect of other religions.

2.1. Developing the Historical Method in the Domain of Judeo-Christian Religion

The history of religion school emerged from the struggle against a one-sided literary criticism that holds sway because of laziness, despite its

---

63. See Hermann Gunkel in the *Deutsche Literaturzeitung* 25 (1904): 1109; also now the foreword to his *Reden und Aufsätze* (Göttingen: Vandenhoeck & Ruprecht, 1913).

obvious shortcomings. In itself, literary criticism is perfectly justified, whatever its special emphasis may be, in order to anticipate any recurrent misunderstandings. Without it, it is not possible to pursue any historical research in the particularities of Old and New Testament traditions. But one must not think that the historian's work is done by engaging in literary criticism. Most literary critics fail to take into account the existence of an unwritten history and the necessity to go beyond the literary texts, if you wish to grasp the driving forces behind history. How often is it the case that what is not written turns out to be more important than what is set down. "It is precisely what breathes life into them, what has effect in history, that is, the vital thing about them ... that never finds it ultimate source in books. Rather, it is in the people, in their experiences and ups and downs, and in history that the roots are found."[64] [31] The historian, attentive to people and conditions, stands with the philologist studying the books. A scholar must be both.

Eichhorn too made fun of the "petty mindset, like an actuary's," of those who take the oldest report on the Lord's Supper that can be dug out of the tradition as a true account of the historical occurrence and reject any further investigation as arbitrary. Even Old Testament literary criticism has been content until now to separate and order the sources chronologically, thinking that the task is then finished. But the historian's work is just beginning: the age of the various levels and ideas must be examined, because the age is often independent of any dating of the sources. So often the more recently written account turns out to preserve an earlier stage in the tradition! A further goal is to trace the history of the oral tradition and thus to reveal the first signs of the later development. This process of continually asking questions puts the finishing touches to and in many ways modifies the results of source criticism. Although we are not able to expand on the matter here, literary history finds itself through this process giving just as rich and varied a yield as does the study of the history of religion.

After it had been ascertained just when and in whose writings a particular viewpoint first turned up, the normal thing was to draw the illogical conclusion that the idea in question originated at that time with that writer. Only rarely did it occur to scholars that a concept or material could have a prehistory. This was how they reached conclusions that seem

---

64. Gunkel, *Schöpfung und Chaos*, 238.

quite impossible to us today, such as Zephaniah was the first to have had the idea of a worldwide cataclysm,[65] Amos originated the term "Yahweh Sabaoth," and Zechariah invented the devil.

The New Testament fared no better: the kingdom of God was obviously a concept coined by Jesus; baptism and communion were cultic rituals originating in early Christianity; "becoming one with God" was the mark of a specifically Pauline type of mysticism; the contrasts between truth and lie, light and darkness were of Johannine origin.

The history of religion school took these areas as its point of departure and endeavored to recognize and describe the prehistory of the traditional materials and concepts. Gunkel traced the creation and dragon myths in the Old and New Testaments and painstakingly demonstrated their historical development from Gen 1 to Rev 12. [32] At the same time, Bousset researched the history of the antichrist from beginnings to final vestiges. Eichhorn delved into the problem of the Lord's Supper. Heitmüller assembled a vast collection on belief in names in order to shed light on the term "in Christ." Hans Schmidt used tales involving dragons and people being devoured by beasts to clarify the prehistory of the material in Jonah.[66] Gressmann searched for antecedents to the prophets' traditions on the end of the world and its rebirth. Even New Testament concepts such as those in the Gospels concerning the kingdom of God and the Messiah or Paul's concept of the God-Man (Martin Brückner[67]) and of belief in spirits (Martin Dibelius[68]) were researched with the aim of ascertaining the link with folklore perceptions or to discover their origin.

Now while it may be true that some studies from the history of religion school relate to peripheral formulae and inconsequential material of no real significance for the development of religion, there are many others that treat questions of fundamental import. Or can we call "trifles" the

---

65. [*Weltkatastrophe*]

66. [Hans Schmidt (1877–1953) was Professor of Old Testament in Giessen and Halle.]

67. [Martin Brückner (1868–?) was the author of several books in the area of New Testament studies, including *Die Entstehung der paulinischen Christologie* (Strassburg: Heitz & Mündel, 1903) and *Der sterbende und auferstehende Gottheiland: In den orientalischen Religionen und ihr Verhältnis zum Christentum* (Tübingen: Mohr Siebeck, 1905).]

68. [Martin Dibelius (1883–1947) was Professor of New Testament in Heidelberg. He became well-known for his use of form criticism for research into the Synoptic Gospels and for his involvement in the ecumenical movement. The reference here is to his *Die Geisterwelt im Glauben des Paulus* (Göttingen: Vandenhoeck & Ruprecht, 1909).]

issues around baptism and the Lord's Supper, the virgin birth, the resurrection, mysticism, and Christology? And, in the domain of the Old Testament, studying the eschatological materials in the prophets, the prehistory of the messianic oracles, of the Servant of the Lord, and of the Son of Man—none of these can be called marginal issues. On the contrary, it would be easy to turn the tables and claim literary criticism's treatment of these matters until now is of "only antiquarian interest."

When all is said and done, it is really of little consequence whether some promise in Amos or Hosea is "authentic." In any case, the expectation of a David to come remains a preexilic one, whether clearly attested or not, as may be demonstrated on internal evidence. Just as the hope for the return of Emperor Frederick II in the seventeenth century can hardly have arisen out of thin air, the hope of David's return can scarcely have emerged only in the exilic or postexilic age. There is also an inner logic of ideas of which it must be said that literary criticism is ignorant.

Another question is of immeasurably greater importance: Did the oracles of the prophets have any links with earlier concepts or not? To make a sound judgment of a person's importance, we must first know to what extent that person's thoughts are dependent on previous generations or on contemporary ideas. [33] Otherwise we will be led to false conclusions and a skewed assessment. If we think that Amos or Isaiah originated their eschatological ideas, we need to record willy-nilly the contents of their pronouncements; it is impossible to really know the innermost religious feelings of the prophets. Unless we have some point of contact in the tradition, we are compelled to regard prophecy as being simply a supernatural quantity that has fallen from heaven. To hold such a view, it is necessary to give up any pretense of historical understanding, of scholarly research. Even here we see the effects of a stage of philology that has been superseded by the present: anything that cannot be found in the ancients has no existence.

How long we believed, under the influence of the doctrine of inspiration, in the linguistic creativity of the New Testament writers! No doubt the simplest soul today can spot how invalid this idea is, because we can prove the contrary from the papyri and the inscriptions "in black and white." But we must be under no illusion what horrible consequences followed from the fact that this false, unhistorical view was uncontested for so long. It led to the New Testament writers being hailed as geniuses of linguistic creativity! Although we may all laugh today at this naïve view,

it is considered valid from a scholarly perspective to say that the prophecies were something absolutely new in their time. Yet we only need to
transfer a recognized truth about language across to the realm of ideas
to see straightaway how untenable this stance is. For like the words, the
thoughts and material have clearly had their own prehistory. To ignore
this prehistory or consider it inconsequential will of necessity lead to
absurd conclusions.

Now, our opponents make fun of our interest in "fossils" and "flourishes," but what is meant as criticism is in fact praise. For historians have
an open mind to everything, not only to grand, earth-shattering ideas but
also to insignificant thoughts and even to worn-out turns of phrase and
petrified formulae. Historians know that these too have had a history, and
it is the duty of those who study history to scrutinize it. There is much
to be learned from the careful study of fossils, and that includes learning
how living beings developed, without having to fall into the blatant error
of those dilettantes who confuse fossils with living beings.

Of course, not all the topics mentioned get right to the heart of religion. [34] However, the secondary results alone have made a decisive
contribution to a reshaping of essential elements of the accepted picture of
Israelite and Christian religious history. It is no longer possible to ignore
the success that has been achieved: historians are erecting a sound edi-
fice from a range of often unlikely stones. It is also easy to see why the
history of religion school has in fact started with those issues that are of
secondary importance. Scholars had until now virtually neglected them
and contented themselves with a few inadequate remarks. They had no
idea that there was a historical problem here because their interests were
confined to philology.

There is no doubt that the question of the history of religion school
means a huge step forward. First, it has opened up to individual historical
research new materials that had never yet been viewed from this perspective. Second, it has provided greater certainty for tentative interpretations.
Linguistic formulae and opinions may be in a state of flux, or they may
have already become set firmly in place, merely being carried over as
traditional material that is not understood. Whichever the case, it is not
possible to reach any certainty about them until we know their history
and their significance in their own times. Things that we could only more
or less guess at have now been removed from the realm of hypothesis and
brought into the bright light of secure knowledge.

Third, exegesis overall has been advanced. If we wanted to convey the meaning associated with an author's statements, we used to be content with a linguistically precise rendition that met the requirements of both lexicon and grammar. Particularly learned scholars would perhaps add a note on the linguistic history of individual words or even venture a new etymology that had absolutely nothing to do with the context. A living language never consists of separate words, but only of words linked together in units of meaning. This was totally ignored, as was the fact that these very units could have very different meanings in different ages.

Nor was any attention paid to the change that occurs in connotation over time, even when the words stay the same. So exegesis that deals with philology and linguistic history needs to be taken further and become exegesis that is concerned with the history of facts and ideas. A concept or a linguistic formula has really been explained only when it has been placed in its context in the overall historical development. Exegetes should pay heed to everything that is necessary to interpretation. [35] This includes fossils and flourishes—most particularly because they appear least comprehensible to modern people, and that is why they demand to be considered historically.

The history of religion school has made it the duty of every scholar to inquire into the prehistory of formulae and materials that were previously totally or for the most part neglected by literary criticism. This is a service none can decry. Now, how far back into history to go is dependent on the individual circumstances. In theory it is the first task of the historian to trace everything back to its origins if at all possible. It is true that there are often impediments to discovery and that true scholarship always remains aware of its limitations. But, as long as any tattered remnants of a veil conceal the final secret, the true spirit of inquiry allows no a priori considerations to block its gaze from piercing even what is apparently impenetrable. Experience has led us to the conclusion that nothing is so alluring as burrowing down to the utmost depths and breaking new ground in places where no foot has ever trod.

However, on the other hand, we must never forget the later developments that overlie the origins. Historians must remove layer after layer with the same care; the first layer must be seen as just as precious as the last. None can close themselves off to the beauty of a flower in all its glory. But just as there is a special charm in watching the sprouting and opening of the buds, it is also entrancing to see the flower fade, shrivel, and gradually die. Nor should we imagine that this work is already finished or even halfway through. On the contrary, it is only just beginning. The motto of the history of religion school is: there is no material in the world that does not have its own prehistory, no concept that does not have links to others. This principle is valid not only for the things that are insignificant and incidental, for formulae such as "thus says the Lord" or for apocalyptic ideas such as "the woman clothed with the sun," but also for the great central themes such as Israelite prophecy or the origin of Christianity. Thus we must ask of all material and all concepts: Where does it come from, and what development has it undergone? Our experience as scholars teaches us how incredibly poor humanity is in concepts and materials, despite all our imagination. What is new is the ever-changing way that light is shed on these things, and this can be of earth-shattering importance.

[36] Now prehistory often lacks any witnesses, and what happened can only be established indirectly. But historians of religion must not shrink from this task either, if they are really seeking historical understanding. Here again the naysayers raise their voice of warning and complain of "subjectivity with no boundaries." Such a criticism comes from timid souls who dare not venture beyond the letter and entrust themselves to the leading of the spirit.

But even conjectural criticism—of which those of a philological bent are usually very proud—can turn into dangerous subjectivism if there is no pioneering spirit of research into language or facts and if the imagination is not held in check by the discipline of a proven method. Now, if these prerequisites are met, no scholar, no matter how careful, will take offense at the spirit being ranked ahead of the letter. Furthermore, the history of language enjoys universal recognition, although it is widely known that it constructs and postulates many forms that have no witness in the literature.

The next thing brought to bear on the methods of the history of religion school is literary criticism, which, although also a product of tradition, is based entirely on faith in the compelling power of logic. Now, if this is not to be written off as mere boundless subjectivity, neither should the history of religion view be taxed with such an objection, since it too builds on the basis of tradition and works by means of logic and psychology. Exactly the same laws apply to it as to every type of historical research. It is not too much to stress that every type of historical writing worthy of the name is a scholarly and artistic construction and is thus distinguished from the writing of annals, which records mere facts and is considered a trade. The motives that are innate to the unfolding of history and its driving forces are nowhere handed down; they always need to be worked out. So no doubt a subjective element comes into historical research, but without such subjectivity historical scholarship has no existence, nor does conjectural or literary criticism.

One particular fear that is held concerning this manner of research is "the tendency to evolutionary constructions."[69] This warning also arises from the lack of a historical viewpoint. The history of religion school regards it as one of its chief tasks to view the various traditions that occur in conjunction rather differently: in perspective as following each other. [37] And that is precisely the weakness in the opponents they are tackling: they do indeed separate the many and various traditions from each other and clearly emphasize where they conflict, but they often rest content with this task, and, further, they leave a whole lot of matters lying on the same level with each other.

As a result of this, it is impossible to gain any historical understanding, which can only be achieved when the traditions are arranged chronologically and an attempt is made to explain how they have changed. This criticism applies even to the great names in historical research, names that we revere. However, the criticism loses its sting when we realize that the method has gradually been refined, which had to happen. Where there is no information, we are perforce reduced to the task of construction, that is, to the internal reasons of logic and psychology. Nor can these at all be chosen at random but can only be determined by the laws that govern everything.

However, all historical research is based on the axiom of development. To deny evolution is to give up any hope of scientific knowledge. Now, experience teaches us that human development never proceeds in a straight line or even in waves. No, it pitches along in juddering jumps. So all sensible researchers will want to remain free of what Jülicher calls "evolutionary superstition."

Still, there is a logical sequence of thought that justifies our organizing data, if not in absolutely, then at least in relatively chronological order. When for example the death of Christ is interpreted as a propitiatory sac-

---

69. Reischle, *Theologie und Religionsgeschichte*, 29.

rifice, then we may claim with certainty that this idea could have arisen only after Christ's death. Historians who are certain of this will not be misled by the fact that this idea was even put into Jesus' mouth. What we have to contend with is not "the tendency to evolutionary constructions," but it is false and one-sided constructions that are the enemy, and they turn up all over the place.

So we need to reject the basic premise, which even Ritschl held to, that the New Testament is to be understood essentially from the Old Testament. This is a view that is almost impossible to comprehend these days; it can only be explained as being dependent on the concept of canon. For historians, the first principle is to deduce every phenomenon from the one that immediately preceded it. In this area the history of religion school again did pioneering work by tearing down the barriers of the canon and opening up a completely new world to research: the literature of the pseudepigrapha and apocrypha. This had previously been the despised Cinderella of biblical study because it lacked any creative personalities. [38] Now, however, it came all at once to be extremely important because it shed light not only on the origin of the early Christian conceptual universe but also on the way Jews of the same period thought and felt. It was only by means of this middle term that it was possible to bridge the gap between the Old and New Testaments and allow for a portrayal of history that actually took into account the continuity of development. Only now can we fill the void that has existed in our knowledge of Jewish spiritual life in the last two centuries before Christ. Again, it was Bousset and Gunkel who were mainly responsible for pioneering new paths in research, and again their books appeared in the same year.[70]

But the history of religion school does not only cast its gaze backwards into the prehistory of the writers and their material. It also looks around at the contemporary history. It is not always possible to distinguish clearly between these two perspectives. Just as the problems of the former arise from an increased historical sense, so also has the latter's quest for the

---

70. Wilhelm Bousset, *Die Religion des Judentums im neutestamentlichen Zeitalter* (Berlin: Reuther & Reichard, 1903), which for the first time showed the historical development on the basis of and in contradistinction to Schürer's "canonical" collection of materials; and Hermann Gunkel, *Zum religionsgeschichtlichen Verständnis des Neuen Testaments* (Göttingen: Vandenhoeck & Ruprecht, 1903), which drew up the broad outline of work for future research.

context evolved from a better historical understanding. There was a time when scholars worried about nothing other than the great personalities of history and were in the habit—no doubt out of ignorance—of overly promoting them for their uniqueness. They took insufficient account of the historical links these figures had with their own past or of the way they were inextricably bound up with their own setting and surroundings. Without paying heed to the overall context, it is not possible to paint an adequate picture of a Moses, Isaiah, or Jesus, a picture that satisfies the demands of religious history: this is the only way to measure the progress they have brought their people.

Of course, these timeless heroes are of such colossal stature that no attempt at description can do them justice. In order to understand them, we must heed the innermost secrets of their personalities. But scholars' senses are sharpened when they are familiar with their surroundings. Scholars too must pay humanity its due from the moment they clothe their thoughts in words that they must borrow, for good or ill, from the world around them. [39] The final goal of historians remains, of course, to understand clearly how original that world is. But if historians wish to go beyond ingenious conjectures and attain real academic knowledge, they need a clear picture of the milieu above which the historical personages tower in all their imposing greatness. Interest in such questions has been aroused only since the awakening of the social sense of modern people. In this respect too the history of religion school is an essential product of our time that would not exist without men such as Taine, Riehl, Naumann, Lamprecht and Wundt.[71] And here we must make mention above

---

71. [Hippolyte Adolphe Taine (1828–1893), French philosopher and historian, was considered, along with his contemporary Ernest Renan (1823–1892), a leading figure in French intellectual life in the second half of the nineteenth century. Although no innovator, he had a great influence on Charles Maurras, Maurice Barrès, and later on Henri Bergson. Nietzsche also admired his work. Alois Riehl (1844–1924) was an important Neo-Kantian philosopher. Neo-Kantianism abandoned the more extreme speculations of the followers of Hegel and advocated a return to Kant's theories. Friedrich Naumann (1860–1919) was a German politician of nationalist and monarchist persuasion and Protestant pastor, as well as founder of the weekly magazine *Die Hilfe*, which addressed the social question from a non-Marxist middle-class point of view. Karl Gotthard Lamprecht (1856–1915) was a cultural and general historian of Lutheran persuasion. Wilhelm Maximilian Wundt (1832–1920), physiologist and psychologist, was a founder of experimental, cognitive, and social psychology.]

all of Deissmann,[72] the pioneer who gave voice to the nonliterary texts of stones, potsherds, and papyri and thus shed "light from the ancient East" on the New Testament.

2.2. Developing the Historical Method by the Introduction of Other Religions

Engaging in research into the overall context led inexorably, of course, to scholars transcending the delimitation of Israelite and Christian religion into the realm of the neighboring religions. This is especially clear when it comes to the origin of Christianity. The first barrier to fall was that of the Old Testament canon; it was no longer possible to ignore the apocrypha and pseudepigrapha. After this the walls of the New Testament canon also came down. Unless one wanted to disrupt the sense of historical development, one could not stop at the last book in the New Testament; the apostolic fathers too had to be taken into consideration. Even Gnosticism itself could hardly be excluded. But the surge of historical knowledge burst all these banks and spread far and wide so that today we are sure of one thing: the apocrypha and pseudepigrapha, together with the New Testament, represent only the tiniest part of a greater overall movement that arose outside the Judeo-Christian sphere in the realm of Near Eastern religions and was only completed by Gnosticism and its relations.

A closer study of Gnosticism has revealed that its origins reach past John and Paul to the Synoptics and even beyond. Gnosticism can be said to be virtually the heir of apocalyptic. The New Testament has one foot still planted in apocalyptic, but the other in Gnosticism. How apocalyptic was replaced by Gnosticism and Christianity's role in that replacement is a topic still awaiting historical research. [40] Historians would need to bring together into one big, clear picture everything that has been proven in individual detail. Then we shall see how right Gunkel was in claiming that many religious themes from other regions were included and transformed in Christianity.

---

72. [Adolf Deissmann (1866–1937) was a theologian, archeologist, ecumenist, and Professor of New Testament in Heidelberg, then Berlin. His contributions to the study of New Testament Greek were seminal; perhaps his best-known work remains *Licht vom Osten* (Tübingen: Mohr Siebeck, 1908; translated as *Light from the Ancient East* (trans. L. R. M. Strachan; New York: Harper, 1910).]

For the study of early Israelite religion it is just as necessary to intro-
duce other religions as it is for Judaism and Christianity. Wellhausen and
his followers have performed a sterling service by understanding the Old
Testament on its own terms and by endeavoring to develop a psychological appreciation of the history of Israelite religion on the basis of the
biblical reports. But since they deduced the opinions of the biblical writers almost exclusively on the basis of internal presuppositions, it is no
surprise that they often went astray. Where they did make a comparison
with other religions, they restricted themselves mostly to Arabic religion,
whose concepts it must be said could only be used by way of general
observation, because there is no question of Israelite religion showing
any dependency in this regard. There were also occasions when some
attention was given to Phoenician religion, of which we know next to
nothing.

On the other hand, the history of religion school avoided such an
error from the outset by spreading its net more broadly and investigating
far and wide the related concepts and influences in the Egyptian, Babylonian, Persian, and, in fact, in all Near Eastern religions. If it be granted
that in many respects it does coincide with Panbabylonianism,[73] in other
ways the two are so fundamentally different that they can only be mentioned in the same breath by the ignorant or the malicious.

The first reason why it is vital to study other religions is in order to
establish analogies. It was Harnack who called the Judeo-Christian religion a compendium of the history of religion:

> If you have been through the way it develops—researching, decipher-
> ing, reflecting and experiencing it all over again—you do not need to
> go and study a whole lot of religions to know what goes on in human
> religion and its history. In the [Judeo-Christian] material you have a
> cross-section that pretty well takes the place of knowing the whole range
> of religious history.[74]

But it was Wrede who provided a decisive refutation to this one-sided
account.[75] The long history of the Judeo-Christian religion, stretching

---

73. [See above, note 58.]

74. Adolf von Harnack, *Die Aufgabe der theologischen Fakultäten und die allgemeine
Religionsgeschichte* (Berlin: Schade, 1901), 12.

75. Wrede, *Vorträge und Studien*, 79.

back thousands of years, does provide an abundance of religious phenomena, but it cannot help us comprehend the real essence of the Chinese religion of ancestor veneration or the Indian salvation religions; there are scarcely any parallels at all. [41] A complete study of the religions of the lower kind of peoples may be undertaken only at their source, no matter how many primitive concepts live on in Judaism or Christianity.

On the other hand, in both the Old and New Testaments, we encounter numerous views that may not only seem strange in isolation but must remain completely without explanation unless some light is shed on them from other religions and they are assigned a place in the history of like or related groups of ideas. We need only recall the concepts of totem and taboo or belief in the power of names and magic, of matriarchies and the worship of the dead, and all the other odd things we have found or claimed we have found in the Old Testament. But even where Judeo-Christian ideas are clear in themselves we need parallels from other areas in order to make a comparison. For it is only these comparisons that enable scholars to grasp the distinctive elements and bring the original into sharp relief. That is why there is no concept or material, no manifestation of Judeo-Christian religion that is excluded from consideration by the history of religion method.

But even at this point we have not reached the end; we are standing at the beginning of a new age of theological knowledge. The greatest merit of the new lexicon *Die Religion in Geschichte und Gegenwart*, edited by Schiele and Zscharnack, in association with Gunkel and Scheel,[76] is to have first clearly recognized and taken up the challenge of this massive task. Although no doubt there are details that must be developed further, nevertheless a solid foundation has been laid. Accordingly, the history of religion school does not limit itself to peripheral matters. It quite simply takes all religious concepts into its purview, so that from now on any general, systematic, or historical research into Christian concepts such as faith, redemption, salvation, worship, edification, resurrection, and so forth that disregards non-Christian perspectives must be considered unscholarly. "If theology really wants to deserve the name of biblical

---

76. [Friedrich Michael Schiele (1867–1913) was a Protestant theologian who became the principal editor of the *RGG* until his early death. Leopold Zscharnack (1877–1955) was Schiele's co-editor from 1910, called in to assist him when his illness progressed. Otto Scheel (1876–1954) was Professor of Church History at Tübingen and known for his work on Luther.]

scholarship"—or even of scholarship at all—"it must go about its task as scholarship *of religion*."[77]

But within the realm of general history of religion it is essential to pay particular heed to those religions that have historically come into contact with the Judeo-Christian religion. That is why the study of Near Eastern religions is especially important. [42] Now, when chairs of religious history in theological faculties are established or fall vacant, it must be a requirement that the scholars who are called to these positions be familiar above all with the religions of the Near East, since it is these that have the greatest significance for the history of the Judeo-Christian religion. What has been happening hitherto does not fulfill all justifiable claims made on it. Of course, at present everyone who pursues the development of Israelite religion must also have a knowledge of the neighboring religions in order to determine what analogies and dependencies there may be. This is likewise true of New Testament scholars and Assyriologists.

But such comparative study of different religions can proceed only in a haphazard fashion, and there are vast areas of the Near East that are almost totally left out. Among these we may number the Hittite religions of Asia Minor and the later syncretistic religions. Only a few amateurs and dilettantes, such as the panbabylonians, romp in these fields. What we need are people who pour all their strength into systematically researching the historical contexts of the Near Eastern religions and see it as their life's work. We need individuals who combine a thorough training in philology with a firm mastery of comparative methodology in the field of the history of religion.

Christian theology has a real stake in this claim, for it is an absolutely intolerable state of affairs when theology is pushed from this field, where at issue are the origins and the originality of Israelite and Christian religion, into a area of secondary importance that must then exist on handouts from the Assyriologists, Hittitologists, and other philologists or even from dilettantes. Granted, the chief task of theologians must be Old and New Testament research, but theology as an academic discipline neglects at its peril the issues that have recently emerged in the history of religion.

---

77. Ernst Gustav Georg Wobbermin, *Die religionspsychologische Methode in Religions-wissenschaft und Theologie* (vol. 1 of *Systematische Theologie nach religionspsychologischer Methode*; Leipzig: Hinrichs, 1913), 111. [Wobbermin (1869–1943) was Professor of Systematic Theology, mostly in Berlin.]

So the principal goal is not to collect analogies and pile up parallels; it is a question of the historical context of religions and the influence they have on each other. To answer this question needs not only particular tact but above all a sure method. The basic principle must be first to understand the psychology of a religion against its own developmental background. It will be psychology that always has the last word in the study of the development of the human mind and spirit[78] and, as a consequence, in the realm of the history of religion.

But there are false psychological constructions and there are true ones. [43] Historians can harbor only the greatest mistrust toward the prevailing "psychological" method of today, since it is used to make the impossible possible. We may shed light on this by an example. In order to explain the idea of the resurrection, which is mostly linked with the concept of judgment, it is customary to point to the human hope of experiencing after death some balance between our piety and our fate, a balance that is denied us in this life. Now, it should be clear after a little reflection that nothing is really "explained" by this. First, resurrection and judgment are two completely independent concepts that must thus also be considered separately when one asks about the origin of things.

Further, it is possible to get a clear idea of the resurrection only when you hold it over against the idea of immortality. The latter word means the immediate continuation of the soul after death; resurrection, on the other hand, means the miraculous regeneration of the body after death, whether the time lapse be brief or longer. In order to be seen as correct, a psychological construction would above all have to take this distinction into consideration and attempt to clarify it. We can take comfort in the claim that there is no psychology that can manage this straight off. Even before making a start on the task, it must carefully set out the individual peculiarities of the historical facts, otherwise the psychological reconstruction will hang in thin air.

The history of religion school requires complete dedication to and correct use of the psychological method. The task of the latter is not only to show how any change in religious views must necessarily come to fruition out of inner motives; it also has to ascertain where an old thread breaks

---

78. [I have reluctantly resorted to a lengthy paraphrase in an attempt to render *Geistesgeschichte*, which refers to the hidden, yet real forces that underlie any period of a people's development.]

off and a new one begins. Just as important as continuity of development are the ruptures and sutures that must not escape the notice of the alert observer. To stay with the example given above, the task of the historian would consist in proving that the Jewish belief in the resurrection, when viewed objectively, turns out to be the continuation of the belief in Sheol held by the early Israelites.

Furthermore, psychology would need to analyze the two worldviews and ask whether the later one is an organic continuation of the earlier. Since this turns out to be impossible, we have to accept a break in the chain of developments at this point. Now, such a rupture points necessarily to external influence. In this case, Judaism's dependent status is clear, whether or not we are able to give a name to the religion that has brought the external influence to bear. [44] Thus, no matter what view is adopted, psychology has to investigate the extent to which this view conforms to the religious development of a people. In addition, it has to consider whether the idea agrees with the economic circumstances or fits in with the geographical position, and in general, what conditions would make it plausible. For just as every plant needs a type of soil in which it alone can flourish, and just as each plant takes on a different form according to the climate, so each idea requires definite conditions without which it cannot grow or develop.

In order to reconstruct the contexts in which religion develops, it is usual to begin with analogies drawn from various peoples. The issue revolves around using this information properly. On the one side we have the followers of Bastian's collective ethnic theory,[79] who tend to see all comparable advances in religion as being derived from a parallel development of the human race. Here they miss the influences, which are basically undeniable, that one religion had on another among peoples who were geographically close or had historical connections.

Those who defend the theory of population shift fall into exactly the opposite error. They incorrectly dispute the spontaneous generation of individual, that is, primitive, beliefs in various places. They consider that there was only a transfer of ideas, and they try to find a single location

---

79. [Adolf Bastian (1826–1905), a pioneer figure of modern German anthropology, developed the theory called *Völkergedanken* (roughly, "ethnic thought"). Bastian wrote prolifically but did not produce a clear final version of his thought. The basic idea was that there must be some elementary structure that underlies the whole diverse range of cultural creativity. The concept of the individual thinking human being was not the key; instead, this formed part of a much bigger picture.]

from which the ideas originated. This location is subject to the whims of fashion: yesterday it was India, today it is Babylon, and tomorrow it may move to Egypt. The history of religion school has distanced itself from both extremes, despite frequent accusations to the contrary by its opponents. The school has always taken the basic view that both comparable developments and historical dependency must be recognized and that a clear distinction must be made between them.

Just as in the case of psychological deductions it is customary to assume continuity with the closest material and to have to specifically justify any break, it will be equally necessary to first attempt an explanation from the natural sequence of development of any material before pleading foreign influences or idea transfer. External witnesses, factual echoes, and even direct terminological resemblance are not in themselves enough to demonstrate a foreign origin, since all of these may be instances of accidental similarities. This is especially true in the case of agreements between primitive concepts and simple ideas, which can emerge anywhere in the world, given similar conditions.

[45] Absolute dependence can be claimed only on the basis of internal logic and psychology. Further, if one places pronouncements of specific religions beside each other in their historical context, then it must be a further requirement that at least the possibility of such an influence be demonstrable. We need the presence of geographic and historic links that lead from one religion to the other. For example, anyone positing a Babylonian origin for Mexican or Chinese ideas need not be surprised to have such theories treated as dilettantish; no more should someone who has derived medieval views attested in Germany directly from Babylon.

On the other hand, in the case of neighboring peoples linked by a common history, one is predisposed to turn features that show similarities into ones that show dependency. This is especially true of the peoples of the Near East, who have been shown to have engaged in mutual exchange of culture and ideas since the third century before Christ. Where there are unusual details that rise above the primitive level, or even agreement between striking combinations of different sequences of ideas, we are most probably justified in suspecting historical influence. We may presume as a rule that such influence has been exercised by the older and more dominant people upon the later, less dominant one.

However, such considerations cannot take us beyond the realm of the merely probable; only internal reasons are of decisive force. Again, let us take the resurrection as an example. It emerges at a time when Judaism was or had been subject to Persian hegemony. Now, the concept of the resurrection is in itself such an unusual idea that the possibility of two peoples independently happening upon it seems excluded from the outset. Since precisely the same view has been confirmed in Persian religion, and since the Persians ruled the Jews, the idea of a Persian origin naturally comes to mind. This probability becomes stronger when we note that the concept of resurrection in both Judaism and Zoroastrianism[80] is intimately connected with the whole eschatological worldview. Therefore, it is not only a detail that agrees, but a striking combination of details.

Despite having reached such a high level of probability, we can talk of certainty only when the results of psychological research show that the idea of the resurrection in Israel makes no sense as a result of internal development but makes perfect sense in Persia. [46] Thus the case can never rest on externals, no matter how well they agree—for example, the legend of the flood or the prophetic oracles. The similarities in terminology between the flood in Babylon and in Israel do not compel us to assume dependency as much as does, to take an example, the way both peoples attribute a combination of wisdom and piety to the main protagonists in the flood story, or the way such wisdom is shown in the identical motif of sending birds out on a mission of reconnaissance on three occasions. However, even such similarities are not decisive, since they could be based on coincidence. The decisive factor is the psychological consideration that no flood myth could have developed in Israel, a people based exclusively on dry land and quite different from the Babylonians. Those who claim that the prophecies in Israel are dependent on the wisdom sayings of the Egyptians must not limit themselves to demonstrating the admittedly remarkable and comprehensive similarities between the forms of those sayings. They must also show that good psychological reasons cannot be given for the Israelite prophecies and that there are at least some of them that remain inexplicable, a fact that would point to a foreign origin.

However, research into the history of religion must not cease at that moment when a definite or even a probable borrowing has been established. It pursues the equally important question of how what was

---

80. [*Parsismus* in the German, but "Parseeism" tends to evoke the further development of these ideas in a religion in India, so "Zoroastrianism" better captures Gressmann's intent.]

borrowed from elsewhere is transformed into an essential part of the new religion, for mechanical borrowings are very rare and can in general only be expected among folk beliefs, although even here one may observe a process of integration, especially over a long period of time. But we may say it is a rule that the major historical figures are masters of and not subject to tradition, either local or imported.

As important as—in fact more important than—the agreements are the variations, because there we see the clearest reflection of the original way of life. At the same time, we must be on our guard against wrongly evening out differences. There are identical forms of words that have a completely different meaning from one religion to another, according to context. On the other hand, there are contradictory formulae that seem to have nothing in common but that go together, for borrowing is most commonly done in the shape of antithesis. Here again we must prize the spirit rather than the letter in order not to do violence to the individual expression.

[47] The history of religion school has come to the firm conviction that great individuals are intimately linked with the world that surrounds their people without in any way denying the individuality or the greatness of these persons. The school is equally persuaded that religions, even the great religions of the world, have historical connections with one another, without any thought of disputing the individuality of these religions. It is the task of historical scholarship to give equal weight to the study of both these aspects. Without doubt the problem of originality is more important than that of dependency, yet the issue of originality can be resolved only after we have answered the question of dependency.

2.3. The History of Religion and the Psychology of Religion

The history of religion school, hotly contesting the facts, is at pains to shed light on the historical development of Judeo-Christian religion. Investigation of other religions also serves to advance this program. Such investigation is not generally an end in itself in theology; it only occurs for the purpose of comparing or proving the historical context. It is unnecessary to delve further into the scholarly presuppositions involved. The only thing that needs emphasizing is that for theological historians the valid basic principles are no different from those that apply for secular historians (of course, *mutatis mutandis*). Just as secular historians must have a close relationship to any time, nation, or historical personage they are studying, likewise historians of religion need to have a profound understanding of religion. In particular, the theologian must have a reverent love for the Judeo-Christian religion. Without such personal involvement, whether it finds expression in the work produced or not, there is absolutely no hope of any sympathetic historical research taking place.

It is no longer necessary to look for "scholarship without presuppositions" in the sense of being free from church dogma, since such dogmatic approaches have been overcome within Protestant theology and can no longer act as a restriction on historical work. As it happens, however, all scholarship, just like art, is awash with presuppositions. Nor is it possible to make any progress without value judgments, since we must constantly compare the various levels of development with each other in order to distinguish the earlier from the later levels.[81]

[48] To make absolute value judgments and answer the question of the truth content of religious ideas is a matter for the systematic theologian. However, historical and systematic theology cannot exist independently of each other, even if they mostly cohabit like siblings at loggerheads, each inhabiting its own domain. But at the points where they cannot avoid coming into contact, it is easy for sources of friction to develop and for these to lead to feuding. In general, historians must avoid invading the domain of the systematic theologian; they will feel themselves to be not entirely at home, as though on foreign soil. So if I nevertheless embark on a little sortie here, because the subject seems to require it, I beg the reader's indulgence in advance.

It will be above all from the older disciples of Ritschl that we can expect objections; the history of religion school arose partly in opposition to Ritschl, quite simply because its adherents believe his reconstructions of history to be in error. In order to anticipate any misunderstanding, let it be stated clearly that no attempt is being made to diminish the value of Ritschl's powerful personality, which captivated a circle of outstanding people. Nor is there any dispute about the liberating power of his theology.[82] We also gladly acknowledge his energizing influence on the

---

81. "But all this is to do with determining relationships," as Jülicher rightly said in his Rectoral address ("Moderne Meinungsverschiedenheiten über Methode, Aufgaben und Ziele der Kirchengeschichte" [1901]); "historians may use endless comparatives in their judgments; on the other hand, strictly speaking, they must never use a superlative."

82. So gratefully celebrated by Reischle, *Theologie und Religionsgeschichte*, 20.

historical study of theology. Nevertheless, his view of history was unten-able, both in its details and in its general outline. He made the concept of the kingdom of God, seen from an ethical standpoint, into the cen-terpiece of his dogmatics, while, although it must be granted this did not occur until after his time, men such as Johannes Weiss, Bousset, and Wrede demonstrated the historical validity of the contrary opinion: the purely eschatological nature of the kingdom. Ritschl did violence to the historical facts. He was misled into doing this by his systematic effort to derive from the New Testament a yardstick that would be free from any limitations imposed by historical time periods and that would also serve as an authority for today. As a dogmatic theologian, he brought to this task a disproportionate perspective that prevented him from making an unbiased evaluation and taking an overall historical view of the New Tes-tament tradition.

But the history of religion school must also raise a note of protest against another, equally important aspect of the position adopted by Ritschl and those theologians he influenced. [49] For Ritschl, the reli-gious worldview of early Christianity was paradise lost, become paradise regained in genuine Lutheranism, and established once more, for the third time, by Ritschl. The periods in between were for him low times, when religious knowledge declined into atrophy. Of course, this is only a sketchy outline of Ritschl's view, which really needs to be toned down, given more delicate nuances and softened, but its basic elements are ren-dered here to show that it leaves no room for a more insightful historical understanding. Lagarde, Eichhorn, and Pfleiderer are right to agree on this point. Those who consider the whole development of the Christian religion since the days of early Christianity until the time of Luther as one single great regression and wish to interpret the "essence of Christian-ity"[83] only on the basis of early Christianity are not in a position to assign sufficient value to the more recent, positive, and creative forces that have added to the picture over the course of history.

It had become customary, despite all their differences of individual viewpoint, to lump together Jesus, Paul, Augustine, and Luther as being, on balance, of one mind—at the expense of historical truth. Then the

---

83. [The title of Ludwig Feuerbach's book. See *Das Wesen des Christentums* (Leipzig: Wigand, 1841), the 2nd edition of which was translated as *The Essence of Christianity* (trans. Marian Evans; London: Trübner, 1881.]

historical sense surfaced, finding its expression in the history of religion school, and noted that there were extensive distinctions to be made. Wrede placed Paul beside Jesus as the second founder of Christianity and showed the deep division between the perspectives held by the two. To make the views of Augustine and Luther agree with Paul's doctrine of justification is like trying to square the circle. So, as a logical extension of historical studies, the solution for our present age was announced: We are free from the theology of early Christianity and the Reformation! Every epoch has its own view of the essence of Christianity, and what is good for the past must also be good for the present. People of today, schooled in history, are fully aware when they demand to do what earlier generations did in ignorance, subject to internal and external pressures as times changed.

Of course, systematic theology cannot do without a historical undergirding. When systematics, like all theology, takes its bearing from the study of religion, it will get in closer touch with history of religion research and be superbly fitted to round it out.[84]

[50] The hesitation one feels in viewing the above ideas is more apparent than real and is only based on the confusing terminology used. According to Wobbermin, it could appear that the history of religion perspective excludes that of psychology of religion, as though they stood in opposition to each other like a historical and a systematic "method." In fact, one perspective cannot exist without the other. It must be admitted that the history of religion school does not treat the problems of the psychology of religion in themselves, only considering them case by case as they are linked to the various empirical facts of religion. In fact, we can go a step further and say that, even with this reservation, the question of the psychology of religion has been unreasonably neglected by the history of religion school. The development of the psychology of religion method, which must be required in the area of historical work, would form a

---

84. This is best seen by considering the term taken up and developed by Wobbermin: "psychology of religion method." He has explained it more fully in his recently published *Systematische Theologie* (Leipzig: Hinrichs, 1913) [see note 75 above]. While the perspective of the history of religion remains entirely within the framework of historical work, Wobbermin's so-called "psychology of religion method" begins where the history of religion approach left off and deliberately goes beyond (440). The task of Wobbermin's method is "to reveal the decisive, basic motifs and tendencies inherent in the forms of expression we see in religion" (403).

middle term for the development of systematic theology from a psychology of religion viewpoint, such as is being called for by Wobbermin.

Since both fields of scholarship have the same aim, they should support, motivate, and complement each other. Research in the history of religion remains at the level of the individual, chance phenomenon, historically contingent. First it examines the historical development of a phenomenon and then it analyzes it right down to the last psychological detail. In the case of complex quantities or of intricate groups of concepts of a whole level of religion, it is the duty of historians to separate the ideas found together without distinction at the same level and to rank them in such a way that what is vital is in the foreground and the incidental phenomena sink into the background. At every juncture, historians must break through the shell to the kernel beneath, trace the creative force behind the conceptions that conceal it, and bring out what is essential from the multitude of ideas. [51] In this way they will ease the task of the systematic psychologists of religion, going beyond the incidental and empirical forms of expression of individual religious phenomena to reach the grand motifs that underlie all religion and the Christian religion in particular.

So it is to be hoped that systematic theology, which until now has mainly been inimical toward the history of religion school, will gradually show itself better disposed and that both of them will work together on the great task set before Protestant theology, using modern scientific methods. The final goal of all our efforts is to shed light on the essence and the truth of the Christian religion. We know we are one in this endeavor with scholars of preceding generations, on whose shoulders we stand, and with those of the present, wherever they happen to be placed in the conflict of opinions. Apart from that, the adherents of the history of religion school go their own way, firmly convinced that the church in this "history of religion" stage of scholarly work needs them and them in particular, in order, in changed circumstances, to reach the age-old goal using new means.

THE LORD'S SUPPER IN THE NEW TESTAMENT

by Albert Eichhorn

Originally published as *Das Abendmahl im Neuen Testament*. Hefte zur "Christlichen Welt" 36. Leipzig: Mohr Siebeck, 1898.

Prefatory Remark

[3] This publication reproduces the substance of a lecture that I gave here in Halle at the Theological Academic Society.

—The author, Halle

[5] I would like to begin with two remarks. My explanations will disturb and displease many of you; there are things that may even offend some of you. I can perfectly well understand such feelings, but it is not possible to completely avoid offense. The matter of the Lord's Supper is no different from other topics in dogmatic theology: the theologian has to learn to face the truth resolutely and courageously.

There is another comment I would like to add. I do not labor under the delusion that I will convince you, since my method of proceeding will not be the customary one. Nor do I have any cause to engage with the opinions of recent years on our topic. You are perfectly free to accept or reject my method and my results. I shall say openly that in the case of such rejection I shall not feel very upset. I feel quite comfortable in my isolated academic position.

In 1876 the topic of the Lord's Supper was treated in the Student College at Erlangen, on which occasion Zezschwitz[1] shared the following reminiscence with Harless.[2] In a lecture at Leipzig, Harless had put for-

---

1. [Gerhard von Zezschwitz (1825–86) was Professor of Practical Theology at Erlangen.]

2. [Adolf von Harless (1806–79), a brilliant scholar and professor of ethics and exegesis in various universities, preacher, church leader, and president of the Chief Consistory of the Lutheran Church in Bavaria, is considered to be the founder of the movement called *Erlanger Neuluthertum* (Erlangen New Lutheranism), which breathed new life into Lutheranism in Germany. As such he was perhaps the best-known representative of nineteenth-century German Lutheran church life.]

ward the idea that the first Lord's Supper was not a Lord's Supper at all, that is, that the disciples had not received the body and blood of Christ. Shortly after that there was a talk in the theological society in Leipzig on the topic of the Lord's Supper at which Harless was present. The speaker made the point very clearly that even the first Communion was a genuine Communion.

> When Christ himself is giving out the bread and the wine and saying the words himself, "This is my body, this is my blood," if these words do not mean that the disciples are receiving the body and blood of Christ, if these words have another meaning, then of course later on, when Christ's words of institution are merely quoted, the words cannot have that meaning either. [6] Conversely, if Christ's words in the church's celebration of the Lord's Supper guarantee or cause his body and blood to be received, despite all rational objections, then of course the words had the same effect when Christ spoke them originally. The Lutheran doctrine of the Lord's Supper collapses if the famous words τοῦτό ἐστιν from Christ's own lips did not have the full force that the Lutheran church attributes to them.

If I remember correctly, this is more or less how the student argued, and the argument impressed Harless. The next time he gave an interpretation in the area of dogmatics, he had altered his earlier view and now said that the first Lord's Supper was an authentic one in the sense adopted by the Lutheran Church.

I have recalled Harless here so as to bring out clearly the point of the matter, which I would like to frame as a question: Is the occasion of which the Synoptic Gospels and Paul speak the first celebration of Maundy Thursday, or is it the first Good Friday sermon, that is, the interpretation of Christ's death?

1. THE LORD'S SUPPER: THE FIRST CELEBRATION OF
MAUNDY THURSDAY

As far as I can see, critical theologians deny the first celebration of Maundy
Thursday, in the sense that Jesus and his disciples believed he was distrib-
uting and they were receiving his body and his blood. To put it briefly, it
is considered impossible in the circumstances for Jesus and his disciples
to have held or to have been in a position to hold such a view. So the
reports as we have them are searched for the real meaning of the act and
the words spoken at the time.

In my opinion, the historico-critical method is deficient. By this I
mean the method that simply takes those reports as historical narratives
that reproduce more or less exactly the actual course of events and that are
to be corrected through the process of comparison until we have reached
the earliest tradition and thus the true historical course of events (both
of these are identified). This is where the history of religion method must
intervene. My question is this: How did the Corinthians and the original
readers of the first three (Synoptic) Gospels understand the reports? Obviously like this: the inauguration of the Lord's Supper was being reported
to them, for the Lord's Supper was a Christian celebration of long standing, the center of Christian worship.

There can be no doubt about this view held by the first readers, and the
writers meant exactly the same thing. It can be demonstrated directly from
Paul, who speaks of the church's Communion as he introduces his account
of its history. I find it impossible to come to any agreement with anyone
who opposes the weight of this fact by saying that he is simply ignorant of
it. The text as it stands cannot be interpreted as meaning that Jesus said or
meant just anything at all *except* the instigation of the Lord's Supper. Of
course, it is quite another thing if the text is considered not to be historical and the contemporary view is held to be at the very least influenced
by Christian worship. [8] In this case, one would be within one's rights in

putting forward an appropriate hypothesis. However, the text as it stands gives no justification for that. I believe the differences between the four texts Matt 26:26–28; Mark 14:22–24; Luke 22:19–20; 1 Cor 11:23–25 are of no great significance. A trial could be made with a modern reader. We are all used to the text quoted in church at the celebration of the Lord's Supper, which is fairly heavily based on Paul. Nevertheless, when all four texts are read one after the other, no one is in doubt that all four are reporting the same material with the same meaning. Yet people of today are disadvantaged by being accustomed to reading one standard text. In the early days, as we see from the variety of texts, there was no such standard text having the same readings right across Christendom. How could the first readers have determined otherwise than that every passage was about the Lord's Supper with which they were familiar?

I shall return to the question of the variant readings. They are of great importance in that they show us that we are not in possession of a simple historical report, rather that the influence of the church's worship is visible at every stage. So the variant readings prove the important thing: that what we have in the biblical reports is nothing other than the Lord's Supper as celebrated in the church. Thus our result is this: Matthew, Mark, Luke, and Paul are telling us about the inception of the Communion in the church.

2. The Lord's Supper: The First Reflection on Good Friday

What is striking in the three Synoptic Gospels is that Jesus says almost nothing about the meaning of his death for salvation, a meaning that was of fundamental importance in the Christian church from the very outset—at least that is the testimony we have in the New Testament letters. This is even more striking because it contradicts the reconstruction of the picture of Jesus handed down to us as we read it in the Gospels.

It is possible to distinguish three different views of Christ's death in the New Testament. The simplest and most natural one is that the death of Jesus is not his actual messianic act. Rather, his death is an act of violence perpetrated by human beings by which, as it appears, an end is made to belief in his messiahship. But God raised him from the dead and thus made him Lord and Christ (Acts 2:36; 10:39–40). So the death of Jesus is the dark background against which the majesty of the resurrected one shines forth even more gloriously. A human act stands over against the act of God.

It can be objected that these speeches were made to non-Christians, and so this view of Jesus' death is the obvious one. It is claimed that only in the speeches of the apostle Peter do we find just this Christian view presented and that there was nothing to prevent the death from being portrayed as necessary for salvation. In fact, the whole dramatic tension of the Synoptic Gospels is based on Jesus' death having destroyed all hope. The disciples on the road to Emmaus express this: "But we had hoped that he was the one to redeem Israel."[3] It is only the resurrection that restores their faith. So too in the whole of the New Testament the resurrection of Christ is the real basis for faith in him. Here we could mention Jesus'

---

3. [Luke 24:21, NRSV. All Scripture references will be to this version unless otherwise stated.]

words to the women of Jerusalem: "For if they do this when the wood is green, what will happen when it is dry?"[4] But this must be said: judgment rightly affects sinners and the unrighteous; the righteous one really ought to be spared. [10] I do not wish to infer from this any more than can be inferred. I do not wish to prove that Jesus had only this view of his death, merely that the view that the execution of Jesus was an act of violence is found in the New Testament.

The second view may be expressed as follows: this death is necessary, since it was prophesied in the Old Testament. Jesus says on the Emmaus road:

> "Oh, how foolish you are, and how slow of heart to believe all that the prophets have declared! Was it not necessary that the Messiah should suffer these things and then enter into his glory?" Then beginning with Moses and all the prophets, he interpreted to them the things about himself in all the scriptures.[5]

And when he is taken prisoner he says:

> Do you think that I cannot appeal to my Father, and he will at once send me more than twelve legions of angels? But how then would the scriptures be fulfilled, which say it must happen in this way?" [6]

So it also says in Peter's speech (Acts 2:23) that Jesus was killed "according to the definite plan and foreknowledge of God."

We must not underestimate the importance of this. We could be inclined to think that a fact does not change in character by being foreordained by God, but in the New Testament things are different. If Christ's death is prophesied in the Scriptures, and specifically death surrounded by evildoers (Luke 22:32), then this death is part of his being Messiah. So it is ranked equally with the virgin birth, the triumphal entry into Jerusalem, and so on.

According to the third view, Christ's death has salvific significance in itself. His death is the sacrifice that atones for sin, purifies the conscience, reconciles us to God, and so on. There are many variations on this, but the sacrificial theory is always in the foreground. This view of the salvific sig-

---

4. [Luke 23:31]
5. [Luke 24:25–27]
6. [Matt 26:53–54]

nificance of Christ's death is found in Paul and in all the New Testament letters, whether it be expressly stated or implied. It is typical of this view that less is said of Christ's dying or of him giving up his life, and more emphasis is given to his blood; all technical opinions about sacrifice are connected with the blood.

[11] This third view, which is a very well developed one, is the most important. The many and varied forms it has adopted—by no means limited to the concept of sacrifice, but drawing on other kinds of views as well—show how vital it was for the Christian church to gain a positive perspective on the death of Christ.

I am making no claim that these three views followed each other in strict chronological order. The first and second view are closely connected when we meet up with them. It is very likely that this is a very old link, or that the two ideas emerged together. The third view is certainly not the oldest and is based on educated theological theorizing. Otherwise we might just as well consider the concept of the Son of God we find in Hebrews to be older than the simple concept found in the Synoptic Gospels.

It is this third view that we see in the words of institution of the Lord's Supper: "This cup is the new covenant in my blood." The author of Hebrews could also have used these words. My conclusion here is that the reports of the Lord's Supper were influenced by the doctrine and worship of the church.

At this stage I need to depict the general makeover that the tradition about the death and resurrection of Christ underwent. It is a very important and inescapable task to examine under what circumstances changes came about to the historical tradition of Jesus in the Synoptic Gospels. Here it is only possible to touch on this subject to the extent that it concerns the Lord's Supper and the death of Christ. It was not sufficient for the early Christians to understand the death of Jesus, whether it be as a precondition for the resurrection, as a necessary fulfillment of the Old Testament, or as a sacrifice for the sins of the whole world. Equally, the mere fact of the resurrection was insufficient. No, Jesus had to have had prior knowledge of and prophesied his death and resurrection. It was only then that he could be seen to be the Lord of death and of life. This development comes to its completion in the Gospel of John (10:18): [12] "No one takes [my life] from me, but I lay it down of my own accord. I have power to lay it down, and I have power to take it up again."

I shall quote some of these prophecies here:

From that time on, Jesus began to show his disciples that he must go to Jerusalem and undergo great suffering at the hands of the elders and chief priests and scribes, and be killed, and on the third day be raised. (Matt 16:21)

"The Son of Man is going to be betrayed into human hands, and they will kill him, and on the third day he will be raised." (Matt 17:22)

"See, we are going up to Jerusalem, and the Son of Man will be handed over to the chief priests and scribes, and they will condemn him to death; then they will hand him over to the Gentiles to be mocked and flogged and crucified; and on the third day he will be raised." (Matt 20:18–19)

"The Son of Man is to be betrayed into human hands, and they will kill him, and three days after being killed, he will rise again." (Mark 9:31)

"See, we are going up to Jerusalem, and the Son of Man will be handed over to the chief priests and the scribes, and they will condemn him to death; then they will hand him over to the Gentiles; they will mock him, and spit upon him, and flog him, and kill him; and after three days he will rise again." (Mark 10:33, 34)

"The Son of Man must undergo great suffering, and be rejected by the elders, chief priests, and scribes, and be killed, and on the third day be raised." (Luke 9:22)

"See, we are going up to Jerusalem, and everything that is written about the Son of Man by the prophets will be accomplished. For he will be handed over to the Gentiles; and he will be mocked and insulted and spat upon. After they have flogged him, they will kill him, and on the third day he will rise again." (Luke 18:31–33)

I have quoted these passages from Matthew, Mark, and Luke here in the hope of forming an impression that mere references could not create. [13] These passages are completely convincing: what we have here is simply historical narrative, albeit set in the future. What we see is:

1. Jesus being handed over to the chief priests.
2. Jesus being condemned to death.
3. Jesus being handed over to the Gentiles.

4. Details of what occurred: Jesus being mocked, spat upon, and flogged.
5. The crucifixion.
6. The resurrection on the third day.

It is not possible to recount the story of the passion any more accurately in so few words. Anyone who talks of Jesus simply having a premonition about his death, or who claims that all Jesus had was a clear perception that the party of the Pharisees was deliberately and actively seeking his death, has not understood our Gospels.

Such examples could be multiplied. I might mention, for example, the exact prediction of Peter's denial, the parable of the tenants, the sign of Jonah. In Luke 11:30 the sign of Jonah is his preaching to the Ninevites, while on the other hand, in Matt 12:40 it is the three days in the belly of the fish, representing Jesus' three days in the tomb. It is clear from these examples how tradition can be reshaped.

Also of interest in this regard are the words of the angel in Matt 28:7: "'indeed he is going ahead of you to Galilee; there you will see him.' This is my message for you." On the other hand, in Mark 16:7, this is what the angel says: "there you will see him, just as he told you." I assume that the words of the angel in Matthew represent the older tradition. This tradition is so fashioned that the appearances of Jesus himself in Galilee are predicted. I further assume that these words of the angel in their altered form were the occasion for Jesus' words in Mark 14:28: "But after I am raised up, I will go before you to Galilee." Then we have the same words again in Matt 26:32. Only someone totally untrained in critical techniques can find a rationale for two different traditions in Matt 28:7 and 26:32. [14] However, I do not intend to treat the shaping of the traditions any further. Of course, it is not possible to demonstrate completely this shaping of traditions in individual cases. It would be feasible to contradict every verse and equally easily suggest a different explanation from the one I have given. This would give the impression that the very main idea I am proposing can be rocked on its foundations. We can see, and this is my point, how our three Synoptic Gospels are full of the idea that Jesus had a precise advance knowledge of and accurately predicted his death and resurrection. In individual cases we can see as clearly as we could possibly wish how the tradition worked, since the different texts of our three Gospels display both older and more recent versions of the tradition beside one another.

I am aware that my opinion can of course only have any value for those who think it historically impossible for such precise descriptions of Jesus' condemnation to have been pronounced by him. On the other hand, those who have no problem with the recorded prophecies by Jesus, that is, those who think he really said these things, will naturally not have their ideas disturbed in the slightest by my remarks.

However, I cannot help reproaching the critical theologians with whom I have to do. The historico-critical method—at least this is valid by and large—proceeds in a completely negative fashion as it treats the issue I have noted and thus remains ineffective. These words of prophecy are judged to be unhistorical and explained as later accretions and are thus laid aside as having no value. But we must place a positive value on this reshaping of the picture of Christ. The history of religion method shows the way here, since its interest is directed to rounding out the picture of Christianity as a religion. The first thing to notice is the earliest Christian literature, since it reflects the process of the development of the religion. So what is undoubtedly unhistorical is often of more value than what is historical, because the unhistorical material documents for us the progress of the religious process, while the historical material is sometimes kept simply as a narrative recollection without having any real value for the study of religion. It is very important that we recognize the earliest layer of the Jesus tradition that has come to us only in fragmentary form. Mostly it is overlaid by later levels, and it is only by proceeding in a critical fashion that we can uncover the earliest layers. [15] Valuing such a procedure is something we share with the historico-critical method. On the other hand, it is just as important, in fact in some respects more important, to recognize how the earlier traditions have been reshaped and to recognize the value of the results of the entire process.

I would like to make an incidental remark on a particularly foolish feature of historical criticism, one that turns up more frequently than one would imagine. There really exist people who think they have to identify the oldest tradition we can recognize with the process of history itself. They believe that any theologian trained in the historico-critical method must reject the latest reports and accept the oldest ones to avoid being accused of arbitrariness. I admit I find this view extremely limited, so I must simply rebuff it as being totally unscholarly. Critics of this sort have a petty mindset, like an actuary's. Tolerant as I am, I cannot put it more kindly.

Of course, this is how things really were: the same factors within the fixed, literary tradition that have had a recognizable effect in changing the old order have also played a crucial role on previous occasions. I think it likely that the most important changes in the traditions happened in the first decades of the Christian church.

Now the question arises: Why, then, was it the earlier tradition that changed, when it was the one that was historically more accurate? The answer is because it did not meet the needs of the church. In the case at hand, it certainly did tell the story of Christ's death and resurrection, but it did not say that long before in Galilee he had accurately foretold everything to his disciples, down to the tiniest details. So in this respect the matter was simply set straight, and it is this amended tradition that we have in our three Synoptic Gospels. It offered the church a satisfying picture of Christ, one that became the successful one historically.

At this point I would like to make the general remark that New Testament scholarship must not work on the Synoptic tradition only from the point of view of separating the sources. It is much more important to pay attention from the outset to the material and its history. We need to ask which material has been transformed by the faith of the church and what were the underlying motives in play as this occurred. [16] Then we will discover that the transformation went deeper than scholars normally assume. We will also find that this process was not a uniform one in every place. In my opinion, it was the miracle stories and the words of Christ that were altered the least, although even there, as I expressly state, we can see the influence of the faith of the church. The material to do with death and resurrection underwent a far greater change. Likewise, the birth narrative was completely reworked.

Now I shall return to the Lord's Supper. Just as it was insufficient to know that Jesus died and was raised, and thus there was the addition of the aspect whereby Jesus himself predicted his death and resurrection, in the same way it was not enough to know what Christ's death meant for salvation. Jesus needed to have articulated this meaning too. So now we can see why we find in the words of institution of the Lord's Supper the church's final and comprehensive interpretation of Christ's death. We need no longer be surprised that such passages as Matt 20:28 and Mark 10:45[7]

---

7. [Eichhorn has verse 46 here, but the parallel is verse 45.]

appear so out of context. We find in the Lord's Supper everything that we might otherwise have missed.

Now I wish to show how the words of institution of the Lord's Supper relate to death. The words "this is my body" in Mark and Matthew are simply incomprehensible as they stand, if we put ourselves back into the historical situation. They are problematic because they do not treat of Christ's death; they only describe the sacramental offering. In Luke and Paul, the matter is clarified by the addition of "which is given for you" (τὸ ὑπὲρ ὑμῶν or τὸ ὑπὲρ ὑμῶν διδόμενον). The meaning is not "which is given or distributed to you in the Communion" but rather "which is given up to death." So we have here the allusion to the death of Christ, and more specifically, we are entitled to add, in the sense of sacrifice.

Now I shall turn my attention to the cup. Mark and Matthew have: "This is my blood of the covenant that is shed for many," and Matthew adds: "for the forgiveness of sins." Here the reference to death is quite clear, as blood is not shed in the Communion. Luke lacks the mention of the cup. Paul says: "This cup is the new covenant in my blood." I draw your attention to the fact that in the case of the cup, the emphasis is not at all on the blood in itself but on the predicates linked to the cup. [17] Not that it is said or meant that this wine is Christ's blood, but that this blood is shed for many, shed for the forgiveness of sins, that it is the blood of the covenant,[8] the blood of the new covenant. This emphasis is so strong that by dint of a stylistic attraction the predicate of the wine, that is, that it is the blood of Christ, is completely swallowed up by the other predicate, that the blood is the blood of the covenant. That is, in Paul, Jesus in no way says that the wine or the cup is his blood. What he says is that this cup is the cup of the new covenant, which (we may be permitted to elucidate) comes into being by his blood shed on the cross.

It is striking to note that the second part of the Lord's Supper, which treats of the blood, is so much richer than the first. The reason does not lie in the death of Christ in itself, since the shedding of blood plays no role in crucifixion. But the concept of sacrifice is quite different, as it concerns the blood, and nothing else. So in the New Testament, apart from the Lord's Supper, we read only of the blood of Christ, never of his body. All the predicates of the blood that were technical ones in the case of sacrifice

---

8. ["The blood of the covenant" refers throughout the discussion to what is often called "the blood of the old covenant." See Exod 24:8 and Zech 9:11.]

are transferred across and now refer to the blood of Christ. For example, the expression that Christians are sprinkled with the blood of Christ does not come from the disciples' possibly having been sprinkled with the blood trickling down from the cross and from this then being transferred to Christians by way of symbolic or allegorical interpretation. Rather, the sprinkling occurred in the rite of sacrifice and from there made its way into religious language. Thus we have the explanation for the statements at the Lord's Supper, so full of content and meaning, not being linked to the bread or the body but to the cup and the blood.

The result we glean from all this is that the words of institution of the Lord's Supper interpret Christ's death as a sacrifice in the way that this meaning developed in the Christian church. To a certain extent we can offer rigorous proof that the words of institution were altered by the church's faith.

1. "For the forgiveness of sins" is an isolated addition in Matthew. There is no theologian trained in criticism who would accept these words as having been spoken by Jesus. They are a reflection on the meaning of the shed blood, but a reflection that is not identified as such in the addition. Instead, it is put into the mouth of Jesus.

[18] 2. "Of the new covenant." According to Mark and Matthew, Jesus was referring to the blood of the covenant, not to the blood of the *new* covenant. We may take this as a genuine reflection: the covenant is the new covenant. However, in the Pauline text, this is not added to the words of institution as a reflection. Quite the contrary: we are told that Jesus himself said this.

3. "In memory of me." These words are lacking in Matthew and Mark. They are found in Paul and Luke, and in Paul we have the characteristic addition of "as often as you drink." So here we have consideration given to a regularly repeated celebration, and there is no hesitation in putting even this reference into Jesus' mouth. So the various reports still in our possession offer us proof that the account was altered by the church's faith and worship. I am only following the development of these details as documented when I say that the depiction of Christ's death as a sacrificial one is the dogmatic reflection of the church. I have demonstrated that in relation to everything to do with death and resurrection we are clearly confronted with a comprehensive reworking of the earlier tradition. We will not be surprised to find our general observation confirmed at a specific point, that is, the Lord's Supper. The result we obtain from

this is that the words of institution are the first reflection on Good Friday that occurred. This interpretation of Christ's death was so profound and exhaustive that there remained nothing else for the church to add, simply because in these words before us we see the expression of primitive Christian faith.

3. Maundy Thursday and Good Friday

In the first place, I argued that beyond doubt according to our accounts Christ celebrated the first Communion with his disciples, that he distributed the body and the blood to them, and that they ate and drank his body and blood. I next showed that we are dealing with the first reflection on Good Friday, that is, the interpretation of the death of Christ.

What should we decide, then? The answer is that the celebration of Maundy Thursday and Good Friday blend together. If we think purely historically, from the viewpoint of the Last Supper, the reflection on Good Friday is disconcerting and difficult when what precedes and what follows are taken into consideration. However, the reflection is in itself a possible one, for it contains no ideas that cannot be made to work. But how were the disciples expected to imagine the bread to be Christ's body and that they were eating his body, that very body about to be delivered up to death? How could they conceive of drinking his blood, not the blood present in his body, but the blood about to be shed? How could they visualize eating his dead body and drinking his shed blood?

All of this is puzzling and incomprehensible. I would not shrink from the idea of a miraculous eating and drinking, but we have no idea of what miracle we are supposed to accept here. If it is the first celebration of the Lord's Supper that we are to accept, then all the emphasis is laid on eating and drinking Christ's body and blood, and the explanation that the body is to be given up to death and the blood is to be shed drops away into an incidental remark. But we saw that this explanation is of anything but incidental importance.

However, all the difficulties are removed when we take the later viewpoint of the church. The Communion is a partaking of the body and blood of Christ, but the mystery of this body and blood is linked to the fact that the body is given up to death and the blood is shed. [20] That is why, in later celebrations of the Lord's Supper, partaking of the body and blood of

Christ goes hand in hand with the Christian interpretation of the mystery of his death.

The conclusion I draw from this brief reflection is that the dual nature of the Maundy Thursday and the Good Friday celebrations proves the accounts we have to be later ones.

[21] 4. THE REAL BODY AND BLOOD OF CHRIST
IN THE COMMUNION

Up to this point I have assumed that according to the New Testament view there is in the Communion a real partaking of the body and blood of Christ. If our accounts are taken to be historical, then we must naturally require some sort of symbolic interpretation. What I am emphasizing is that no such symbolic view can be justified from our texts. No act takes place that could allow such an interpretation. It cannot be said that the breaking of the bread points to the breaking of the body and the drinking of the wine to the shedding of blood. In point of fact, the act that takes place is simply eating and drinking. At a meal, bread and wine are present for eating and drinking, and it is not a symbolic act when they really are eaten and drunk. The breaking of the bread does not take place to symbolize something but simply to distribute to everyone something to eat. Jesus is merely acting as the father of the house. In the same way, the cup is passed around so that everyone can drink from it. There is nothing symbolic in this procedure. The eating and drinking gain their particular character from the words spoken. The fact that Jesus' words about the meaning of his death are linked to eating and drinking is not rooted in the eating and drinking themselves but must have some other circumstances as its basis. We can think only of the whole nature of the meal when this eating and drinking took place. It was the Passover meal, so the meaning can only be that the Passover lamb is the sacrificial meal of the Old Testament. Now with this bread and wine of which we are partaking at the Passover meal, I am declaring that Passover meal to be obsolete. I myself am the sacrifice of the new covenant; my body is to be given over to death, my blood is to be shed.

Here I would like to warn against any inappropriate erudition based on the Old Testament. [22] Let it not be asked whether according to the Old Testament the Passover meal was a covenant meal, what eating the

Passover lamb signified, and how the smearing of the blood on the door-posts was to be understood. Instead, a well-trained historian must simply assume that all kinds of ideas about the covenant, sacrifice, covenant sacrifice, and sprinkling of blood were linked quite freely to the Passover meal. Of course, the New Testament letters take for granted all sorts of suppositions about the sacrifice that are not developed in the Old Testament. It is my contention that this way of understanding the scene, a historical view, is the only possible one, because it is the only one that fits the situation.

Now, I am not going to discuss the idea that on this view a particular celebration of the Lord's Supper among Christians as a meal in the worship service would really be superfluous, indeed upsetting. If the whole act means only that Christ is the true Passover lamb, and if the eating and drinking at the last Passover meal only has the purpose of showing that such a meal is obsolete through the sacrifice of the new covenant, then it is sufficient for Christ's church to recognize the death of Jesus as a sacrificial death and to remember him in their worship service. On the other hand, there would be no basis for retaining a segment of the Passover meal (for the whole meal is, after all, not eaten in the Christian church) in order to pronounce that this eating and drinking has been made obsolete by Christ's death. At the very least, the view could be explained by saying that when such eating and drinking took place—which for Jesus was only an opportunity for him to give the interpretation of his death—the body of Jesus was eaten and his blood drunk.

We find this realistic version in Paul, for whom the Lord's Supper is not simply a memorial celebration of Christ's giving of his body to death and the shedding of his blood. In Paul's opinion, there is a partaking of the body and blood of Christ in the Communion. The bread is the fellowship of Christ's body and the cup the fellowship of Christ's blood.

Objections can be made to this. Paul is placing the Lord's Supper in parallel to sacrificing to idols. But in such sacrifice the demons' bodies are not eaten nor their blood drunk, so Paul cannot be speaking of a real partaking of the body and blood of Christ. This objection is not valid, for Paul certainly had in mind a more realistic connection to demons than we are inclined to accept. [23] Moreover, an analogy only needs to be valid in certain respects, not in every respect.

It can also be objected that Paul himself offers an explanation of the body of Christ, according to which the body is the church (1 Cor 10:16).

However, it is evident that what we have here is not in the strict sense an explanation of the body of Christ, as we cannot attribute to Paul the idea that Jesus gave his disciples the bread with the words "this is my body, that is, Christendom." The fact is that even for Paul the Communion is an act of worship, a sacramental, not a profane, act of eating and drinking, of the body and blood of Christ in some supernatural sense. Here I need to add a brief general remark on worship and thinking.

In religion, worship makes its own particular claim of independence over against thinking. There is a sensual and a suprasensual factor in worship. As soon as thinking or theory takes hold of worship, it will always turn out that thinking, on the one hand, does not attain the heights of the act of worship, and, on the other hand, it goes beyond worship, makes it more profound and at the same time diffuses it. So it is with Paul. He does not offer any precise explanation that would exhaust the content of the words. Rather, he offers an interpretation that is at the same time a reinterpretation. It takes its purchase from the words "the body of Christ," not from the act of worship itself. In the Communion the body of Christ is given, but Christians too are the body of Christ, and we may use the occasion of many people partaking of the *one bread* to talk of many people having *one body*. It may be said that Paul is making a wordplay here on "the body of Christ." It is clear from the lack of mention of the blood of Christ in counterpoint that we are not to press the thought here too far. The body and the blood are offered equally in the worship service, whereas the possibilities of interpretation they suggest differ according to the various values attributable to the words in the religious vocabulary. "Body" can be interpreted as referring to Christendom, but there is no religious terminology that corresponds to the blood of Christ. Conversely, in the case of sacrificial theories, the term "the blood of Christ" is the only one that can be used; no use can be made of the term "the body of Christ." Thus the words used in the Lord's Supper about the forgiveness of sins and the new covenant relate to the cup, not to the bread.

[24] It can be seen from these remarks that we are not justified in bringing the explanations offered by Paul into the argument alongside the idea of really partaking of Christ's body and blood conveyed by the worship service. We can also see in chapter 6 of John's Gospel that eating and drinking the body and blood of Christ are of significance in the Christian church. What is clearly being discussed here is the eating of the flesh of Christ and the drinking of his blood, as *food*. This is also the way Ignatius

takes it (φάρμακον ἀθανασίας).[9] It is John's Gospel that takes theologizing about Christ to its furthest extent. It will scarcely be surprising that Jesus speaks of the Communion at the time when he is having his most effective ministry. In the conversation with Nicodemus we also see baptism referred to, and John the Baptist speaks of Jesus as the Lamb of God that bears the sin of the world. I only mention John's Gospel here to demonstrate that what is under discussion is a real eating and drinking of the body and blood of Christ. Nothing changes if we try to allegorize or spiritualize the words; this way of speaking would always point to a corresponding use of language in the worship service.

I would like to touch briefly on John 6:63: "The flesh is of no avail." Of course, this does not simply mean the opposite of what has preceded. What it means is that Jesus is not being considered here in his earthly appearance (as σάρξ). As the previous verse shows, his words will only be understood when he has ascended to heaven. I do not wish to deny the notion that eating and drinking of Christ's body and blood, no matter how real we may have thought it to be, also has a spiritual aspect. Thus Ignatius says somewhere that the body of Christ is faith and the blood is love.[10] This fits in with the use of religious language of those circles to which John's Gospel is to be attributed, from the history of religion standpoint.

Now let us turn from Paul and John back again to the Synoptic Gospels. They report quite simply that Jesus celebrated the meal together with his disciples in the way that the Christian church knew it. [25] If the body and blood of Christ were partaken of as supernatural food, then this was obviously also the case when the Lord's Supper was instituted. The Gospels frequently tell us that the disciples did not understand Jesus, even when he was speaking most clearly in a way that anyone could comprehend. If it were in place anywhere, then such lack of understanding would fit in here at the Lord's Supper. But the whole action takes place as being something obvious. Why? Because in the church this celebration with the appropriate words *was* something obvious.

---

9. [Ignatius of Antioch (ca. 35–ca. 107 C.E.), *To the Ephesians* 20.2: "breaking one bread, which is the medicine of immortality, the antidote so that we should not die, but live forever."]

10. [Ignatius of Antioch, *To the Trallians* 8.1: "clothing yourselves with meekness, be renewed in faith, which is the flesh of the Lord, and in love, which is the blood of Jesus Christ."]

We may now sum up our findings. According to our accounts, the inauguration of the Lord's Supper was both a celebration of Maundy Thursday and an observance of Good Friday at the same time. In both respects, both as regards the interpretation of the death as well as of the supernatural partaking of the body and blood of Christ, the accounts are extraordinarily influenced by the worship and the teaching of the earliest Christians.

If our accounts have been altered by later influences to the extent I have demonstrated, then the reader will not be surprised when I add by way of clarification that the original historical course of events can no longer be clearly traced. Up to this point I have ventured observations from a history of religion point of view. In the current climate, these comments are not yet considered to be of scholarly validity. Perhaps I shall have some measure of success in redressing my academic credentials in the reader's eyes if I conclude with a few remarks from a textual-critical standpoint.

From the context in which the accounts of the Lord's Supper are found, even today it is possible to recognize, although somewhat imprecisely, that changes have been made. In Matt 26:29 we read:

"I tell you, I will never again drink of this fruit of the vine until that day when I drink it new with you in my Father's kingdom."

These words are spoken after the meal. (Likewise Mark 14:25, and in contrast, Luke 22:16–19.) Before the institution of the Communion, Jesus says of the Passover meal:

"For I tell you, I will not eat it until it is fulfilled in the kingdom of God." (Luke 22:16)

And of the cup he says:

"I will not drink of the fruit of the vine until the kingdom of God comes." (Luke 22:18)

Only then does Luke have the distribution of the bread.

These words impress us as words of farewell. They link remarkably poorly to the Communion, since they bear no relationship to it. It does not matter whether you have the Communion preceding or following these words. In fact, you can remove the entire account of the Communion from Matthew, Mark, and Luke without leaving any gap.

[27] The words of Jesus that have been quoted would provide a completely fitting ending to the Passover meal, where several cups were drunk by the participants. These words of farewell, which have, as noted, no relationship to the Communion, have been preserved in the tradition. They have not been suppressed, although their positioning has been somewhat unclear, sometimes before and sometimes after the Communion meal. What we have here, purely from the standpoint of textual criticism, is an indication that there has been an intrusion into the earlier tradition of Jesus' last meal.

It would be tempting to prove the uncertainty of the tradition by using the particular instance of the original text of Luke's Gospel. Mr. Haupt,[11] among other critics, has decided to remove Luke 22:20 on the basis of the manuscripts. So Luke is offering us an account of the Lord's Supper without the cup. In the standard text of Luke this gap has been filled by adding the cup in accordance with the Pauline text 1 Cor 11:25. We should recall that in the Acts the Lord's Supper is marked simply by the breaking of bread. When the resurrected Christ goes to Emmaus with the disciples, the distribution of the bread is described as in the Last Supper, and this is how the disciples recognize him. When they are relating this, they stress again that they recognized him in the breaking of bread. It seems reasonable to think that this was a celebration of Communion with the resurrected Christ. This could be offered as evidence that there was an older tradition of the Lord's Supper that mentioned the bread and the body alone, without the cup. So if the cup was a later addition, this would explain the fact that the doctrinal expansion is greater and clearer here than in the case of the bread. However, such a suggestion is too uncertain to be relied on. Mr. Haupt's explanation is very plausible when he says that Luke omitted the cup only because he considered the earlier cup, when Jesus speaks about the vine, to be the cup of the Last Supper.

---

11. [Erich Haupt (1841–1910), member of the ruling consistory of the Lutheran church (Eichhorn gives him the polite honorific title "Herr Konsistorialrat"), was a highly esteemed university teacher and Professor of New Testament at Kiel. He later became *Rektor* (Vice-Chancellor) of the University of Halle. Eichhorn apparently has Haupt's *Über die ursprüngliche Form und Bedeutung der Abendmahlsworte* (Halle: Gebauer-Schwetschke, 1894) in mind.]

I agree with the scholar mentioned above that we must exclude the assumption that Luke knew of a Lord's Supper without a cup.

If the accounts of the Last Supper are not historical, that is, if Jesus neither interpreted his death in the way indicated nor offered his body and blood for the disciples to partake of in the way indicated, then we must ask how these ideas arose. I have already presented my version of the interpretation of the death. There are no problems here.

But how did the idea of eating and drinking the body and the blood come into being? I emphasize that this question must be raised equally by all theologians, whether one doubts the historical nature of our accounts or not. For those who consider the accounts historical must give some sort of symbolic interpretation to Jesus' words. Then those same theologians will find that there arises the question of how the connection to the idea of really partaking of the elements could have come about. So this question is the same for all theologians, except for the few who claim that even in the first Supper the disciples really partook, in the Lutheran sense, of the body and blood of Christ.

The answer to our question can only be that we are not in a position to say. It may be that the Passover meal, and religious conjecture linked to it, seeing Jesus as the real Passover lamb, all served as a catalyst, but we have no real explanation here on the level of the history of religion. The Passover meal is not a supernatural one and so cannot explain the idea of such a supernatural act of eating. In addition, the Lord's Supper has no worship basis in the Passover. It is not celebrated annually; no lamb is eaten. As far as we can see, in Christian scripture it stands alone from the beginning. If we cease to rely on the Passover association, then according to our accounts—and I want to give this its full weight—we lack any possibility of explaining anything. However, there remains this to say: in my view, we can be clear and precise about circumscribing the context within which the answer would have to be found.

[29] I need to add a few quite general remarks here. Both on the whole and in the context of the history of religion, we can meet up with concepts we do not understand and claims that present themselves as self-evident but that to us seem anything but so. The problem is not that we are too stupid but that we lack certain basic knowledge that was common coin to earlier generations. We readily admit this in the case of ideas and viewpoints that are demonstrably very ancient. But not in the matter we are dealing with here, for eating and drinking the body and blood of Christ does not stem from the primeval ages. It is something new that turns up only in the Christian church and had no previous existence—and that makes the matter even more puzzling. The individual concepts of bread, wine, body, blood, eating, and drinking are not difficult. It is precisely the relationships between these concepts that appear impossible to us: in eating and drinking the bread and wine we are partaking of the body and blood of Christ. But the earliest Christians cannot have felt this to be an impossibility; that is, we must assume that there was nothing strange for the people of that time about a supernatural eating and drinking of a heavenly meal in the worship service, giving eternal life. If that was something familiar to them, then the only new thing for the earliest Christians was that some other supernatural substance was replaced by the body and blood of Christ.

A procedure of this sort is frequent in the history of religion, and we have examples of it in the New Testament. Here I may merely point to the death of Christ. From the outset, the only thing we can understand is that it brings judgment upon the Jewish people. What is incomprehensible is how it effects forgiveness of sins for both Jews and Gentiles. But the sacrificial theory in its long-established form provides for all of this. It is just that now Christ is substituted as a new subject, and all of the predicates that quite understandably go with the sacrifice are now transferred with the greatest of ease to Christ.

So all the difficult aspects of the various links between ideas disappear. [30] I would like to add a contemporary illustration here. It is very hard to imagine a person of average intellect and conduct that is far from exemplary being gifted with divine infallibility. But these ideas have taken shape through long historical process in regard to the papacy. If the sort of person mentioned above is now elevated to the papal throne, there is no problem, religiously speaking, in applying all the dogmatic assertions about the papacy to this individual too.

We do not find the necessary conditions for the Lord's Supper in the New Testament, where there is no real sacramental eating and drinking. We will have to have recourse to that type of Near Eastern religious view that I quite simply call gnostic. Of course, I am using *gnostic* in a rather different sense than is customary among church historians. Judaism and Near Eastern Gnosticism run together in the Lord's Supper as they do in baptism. Baptism for the forgiveness of sins is explicable on the basis of the Old Testament. On the other hand, baptism in the sense of being cleansed for new birth with a view to eternal life is Near Eastern Gnosticism. Forgiveness of sins at the Communion is Jewish; the Communion as partaking of eternal life is Near Eastern. In John's Gospel we find that baptism brings about the new birth and that the Communion bestows eternal life. This goes with the practice in John's Gospel of giving a Christian slant to concepts that have had a long history of use in the gnostic religion.

Of course, we cannot prove that a sacramental meal of this kind was the model for the Lord's Supper; this is the gap in our historical knowledge. It is the historian's task to recognize the gaps in our knowledge and to define their limits according to their scope and meaning. Scholarship can do no more than that. It cannot fill in the gaps. The finer the historical sense and training in historical method, the better fitted one is to recognize whether or not one is dealing with a regular historical development. For me, the problem lies in the historico-religious development. Whatever Jesus may have said and done on that evening, I cannot on that basis comprehend the worship meal of the church with the sacramental eating and drinking of the body and blood of Christ, as it seems to have developed pretty well from the beginning among the earliest Christians.

[31] We must accept with gratitude what we are offered by way of filling in this gap. Here I am reminded of Spitta's comments on the Communion.[12] Yet I must make the assertion that none of what we have been taught is sufficient to really provide an answer to the main question. In the last few years there have been numerous attempts at explaining the Lord's Supper; these attempts have proved to be incredibly odd and varied. All of those who provided the explanations believed they were clearing away all

---

12. [Friedrich Spitta (1852–1924) was Protestant theologian and professor in Strasbourg and Göttingen. Eichhorn presumably is referring to Spitta's "Die urchristlichen Traditionen über Ursprung und Sinn des Abendmahls," in idem, *Zur Geschichte und Litteratur des Urchristentums* (3 vols.; Göttingen: Vandenhoeck & Ruprecht, 1893–1907), 1:205–337.]

the difficulties and making everything plain. The historico-religious problem that we are faced with has not been clearly recognized by any scholar.
That is why I have thought it necessary to point out once again what is at
stake, from the viewpoint of the history of religion.

Appendix:
Sacred History*

by Albert Eichhorn

Outline of the Article
1. In the Bible
2. Relationship to the Church
   a. The Catholic Church
   b. The Protestant Church
3. Sacred History Replaced by Modern Theology
4. The "Biblical Basis" and the "Facts of Salvation History"
5. The Problem for Religious People of Today

1. The Old Testament offers a connected story, beginning with the creation and ending with the establishment of the Second Temple community after the exile. It is a product of postexilic Judaism, which, through a process of collecting, sifting, and compiling the available stories, finally brought together and preserved this unified history by establishing the Old Testament canon. We cannot deal here with the literary aspect of this enterprise, whose enormous importance is even today scarcely given its due in theological circles. What is of interest to us here is the fact that this process brought the entire history of Israel, not to mention the history of humanity, into a purely religious focus. And the Old Testament contained ample pointers to the final goal: the fulfilling of Israel's hope, God's judgment of the people, a new heaven and a new earth to bring to fruition the history of the people of God and of the human race. This convinced Israel

---

* Originally published as "Heilige Geschichte," cols. 2023–27 in vol. 2 of *Die Religion in Geschichte und Gegenwart*. Edited by Friedrich Michael Schiele and Leopold Zscharnack. 5 vols. Tübingen: Mohr Siebeck, 1909–13.

that they were in possession of a story that must bear the name of "sacred history" because its beginning, continuation, and end were directly determined by God himself.

The Christian church inherited this tradition and with the story of Christ and the apostles added to it something of equal or even greater importance. Thus we describe the story of the Old Testament and the New Testament as sacred history, which is characterized not only by its religious nature but still more by the supernatural element, classically expressed by the multiplication of miracles.

2. The history of the church is thus linked to sacred history. Here we must emphasize that Catholicism and Protestantism distinguish the history of the church in different ways from sacred history.

a. To put it briefly, Catholicism sees church history as also being sacred history: it is granted that the apostolic period is foundational and normative for all time, but the history of the church continues sacred history—albeit at a rather more profound level—yet with no clear interruption or basic distinction. The history of the church is under God's direct control and will perdure until the end of time; no persecution has suppressed it, nor can it do so in the future. The teaching of the church is without error, a fact that is only brought into particularly sharp focus by the infallibility of the pope. It is a patent error to assert that the popes have ever exceeded the limits of their power. Canon law is by its nature divine law. Thus the history of the church is to be seen from a supernatural perspective. Miracles are an essential part of this history, not only in the sense that the sacrament has a supernatural character, but in the sense that the divine character of the church is constantly attested by miracles. In fact, contrary to a widespread Protestant misconception, it must be pointed out that in no way do miracles belong only to the time of the church's founding. Quite the opposite is the case: even in ancient times miracles are reported more and more frequently from one century to the next, reaching an apogee in the Middle Ages, when they were an almost daily occurrence, and they accompany and attest to the divine character of the Catholic church right to the present day (Lourdes). Direct revelations of God or of the Virgin Mary are equally common.

Protestants often overlook the fact that by placing church history on virtually the same level as sacred history, the Catholic Church is enabled quite unselfconsciously to grant recognition to the various new impulses and institutions that occur over the course of history and to adopt and make them a fruitful part of religious life. The saints appear alongside the characters from the Bible and in religious teaching achieve great significance of their own from the veneration accorded to those heroes. Thus their influence is actually far greater than that of sacred history. In this regard we may think of monasticism, which throughout history right up to the present day has managed to take on ever-new contours by drawing on its own resources. It is now of only theoretical value to claim that monasticism was instigated in principle at the founding of the church. In any case it takes nothing away from such men as Saint Francis of Assisi, Ignatius Loyola and Saint Vincent de Paul that they were born in a later age. It is of very little importance for the new tasks these men set themselves and the church and for the institutions they founded whether it was possible to discover biblical precedents for their activities. That is to say that the biblical sacred history has in practice exercised hardly any restraining influence on the freedom of the Catholic Church. The truth of the matter is that for the Catholic Church the classical period is the Middle Ages and not the apostolic era.

b. Protestantism made a fundamental break with the supernatural character of church history, thus setting religion free from the burden of the past, creating room for new religious goals, broadening the perspective of religion to allow for changes, for ossification and paralysis, for profound insights and innovations—all of which are as typical products of religion as they are of any other human endeavor. This cleared the way for an impartial view of church history, for the modern scientific perception that applies the same criteria to church history as to history in general.

3. The sacred history of both Testaments remained for a time quite undisturbed by this revolution and became even more clearly distinct from any other history. The six-day creation, Balaam's ass, the sun standing still for Joshua—because they were sacred history, these were all immune from any assault, as were the characters of the holy men of God (Abraham, Jacob, and David). Such is the stage where the conflict between tradition and the scientific approach is played out. Since the Enlightenment, the modern scientific study of theology has made particularly sluggish advances into this terrain. Nor has any takeover occurred without numerous compromises and transient truces. At the present time the scientific view of sacred history has prevailed among German theologians; texts and historical traditions are researched and evaluated like any other historical sources. The origin, content, and development of the religion of

Israel are studied using exactly the same methods as are used to study the religion of other people. And no exception can be allowed for the study of the New Testament, the gospel story and the person of Jesus—an exception that is still frequently made with more or less determination and conscientiousness. It is our present task to discover and lay bare more and more of the threads that connect the origin of our religion with the religious conceptions of that time. Such threads are far too numerous for us to isolate that point when the sacred, supernatural history that is clearly distinct from all other events could stake out its territory.

4. The development we have outlined above came to fruition in "modern theology." We must also stress that the particular divine character of sacred history has held its ground unshaken until the present day in wide areas of Protestantism.

(a) There are many and varied attempts to provide a "biblical basis" for all church institutions, for preaching, for the eldership, for the diaconate and the office of deaconess (and the multifarious branches of the Inner Mission[1]). In any case, the questioning of the biblical rationale for any of these was widely taken in Protestant circles to be assailing their legitimate role in the church. When two decades ago the social question began to weigh on people, it was considered right to seek counsel in the New Testament about what position church and state should adopt in regard to these quite modern questions, just as in the Reformation period the case of the Old Testament king Josiah was evoked to show that worldly rulers have the right to issue church ordinances. Yet this is a fairly isolated instance in Lutheranism[2] because Old Testament institutions have nothing to do with Christians (Luther) and because the New Testament is the norm for the doctrine that is in the last analysis the only important thing for the church. Everything else is left up to Christian freedom. However, as was illustrated above, this freedom in principle has been subject to fluctuations right down to the present day. It cannot be denied that constantly referring in this way to the New Testament for the answer to any and all questions that might arise from now until the end of time has lent a certain narrowness to Protestantism, especially Lutheranism, and

---

1. [The Inner Mission (*Innere Mission*) was founded in the mid-nineteenth century to revitalize the Christian witness of the Lutheran church. It concentrated on "saving love"— the expression of piety through good works and Christian education.]

2. Calvinism drew far more heavily on the Old Testament.

contributed to its lack of fruitfulness in regard to new spiritual and social developments—a classic example is Vilmar and his "theology of facts."[3]

(b) However, the main importance of sacred history is found among those circles that, in the ways suggested above, emphasize it over against the whole of history, not as an example of history but as something different. Its true nature consists in the fact that it has secured *the facts of salvation*.[4] The salvation of the world is established forever on certain historical facts, such as the miraculous birth of Christ, his death, resurrection, and ascension. All other facts of the Old Testament and New Testament serve to foreshadow these facts and ground them in the course of history. And these facts are those contained in the Apostolic Creed and celebrated in Christian festivals. These facts serve as the foundation of the Christian religion for church orthodoxy, which for that reason is perfectly entitled to base itself on Paul. For Paul, salvation has been brought about in a drama that encompasses heaven and earth, beginning with the creation of Adam and concluding with the return of Christ. This drama is most decisively expressed in the death and resurrection of Christ, facts that are of suprahistorical character and that bring about salvation. These facts are held dear by the Christian church of all ages and confessions. However, it gives us pause when we reflect that the whole history of dogmatic strife has turned on quite different matters. Even during the Reformation it was claimed that the whole issue was about the essence of Christianity, and no one contested these facts of salvation. In fact, the emphasis on these facts as being the main question in religion is only of recent origin. Schleiermacher deliberately ignored all the facts of salvation; the sheer vitality of the God-consciousness in Christ and its thrilling effect on us—that was the Christian religion, as far as he was concerned. And for Hegel and the theologians of his circle, Christianity was the concept of the unity of God and human being—divine humanity. This concept, found in Christ, developed now in a multitude of directions.

---

3. [August Friedrich Wilhelm Vilmar (1800–1868), after losing and then regaining his faith, became convinced of the deep reality of sin and grace and the supreme relevance of repentance as outlined in article 12 of the *Augsburg Confession*. He was appointed professor of theology at Marburg in 1855 and wrote the influential *Theologie der Tatsachen wider die Theologie der Rhetorik* (1856: *Theology of Facts against the Theology of Rhetoric*), where he advocated the necessity of adherence to the confessions as a whole, not picking and choosing among them.]

4. [*Heilstatsachen*.]

So then, church confessional theology emphasized increasingly strongly, against Schleiermacher and Hegel, that Christianity was not a matter of pious feelings or ideas, nor was it a doctrine. It was sacred history whose realities form the foundation for all subjective Christian piety. Increasingly, church theology gave up developing this idea and returned as its base to the New Testament. Church theology does not see in the New Testament a complex of recent religious movements and ideas going on to produce new forms of religious life up to the present day as it engages in a continuous interchange with new spiritual currents. What the New Testament does contain for church theology is the final and definitive expression of the Christian religion. The facts of salvation form the essential basis for this New Testament religion. The person of Christ too takes its religious significance from those very facts, bringing about the act of salvation through them. The importance of the religious ideas of the New Testament lies in their interpretation of these facts and of sacred history itself. So we are placed in direct contact with the New Testament, in order to assimilate the meaning of these facts. In connection with this we find a total indifference to the further historical development of the Christian religion, since this history has no religious message for us. Such a religious message remains exclusively the domain of sacred history.

5. In his *Critique of Pure Reason*, in dealing with the antinomies of reason, Kant draws our attention to the fact that both the statements "the world has no beginning" and "the world had a beginning in time" can be proved and, conversely, disproved, but that the latter statement is more generally endorsed. This is because human beings recoil from the idea of infinity and need a fixed point of reference. Thus we find that among our squalid huts there arises the cathedral with its message of eternal divine peace, particular days become holy days, and individual actions become imbued with a special blessed significance. So in the unending tide of events, religion has its sacred history where God is at work in a direct and immediate sense and reveals himself directly to us. Even where there is a denial of God's direct intervention today via miracles, as is widespread in Protestantism, this need frequently persists. Those who are so minded believe that the reality of religion is under question when the sacred history is subordinated to the laws of nature and psychology. The answer can only be that the practice of rigorous science and profound religion no longer allows of an external distinction between sacred history, between any special working of God and whatever else may happen in the world.

The ultimate source of the religious impulse lies within the religious person, and the holy ones of both the Old and the New Testaments will always take their place among such people.

Index of Names